Series/Number 07-083

MW00414975

# CENTRAL TENDENCY
# AND VARIABILITY

**HERBERT F. WEISBERG**
*Ohio State University*

**SAGE** PUBLICATIONS
*The International Professional Publishers*
Newbury Park   London   New Delhi

*For information address:*

SAGE Publications, Inc.
2455 Teller Road
Newbury Park, California 91320
E-mail: order@sagepub.com

SAGE Publications Ltd.
6 Bonhill Street
London EC2A 4PU
United Kingdom

SAGE Publications India Pvt. Ltd.
M-32 Market
Greater Kailash I
New Delhi 110 048 India

Printed in the United States of America

Weisberg, Herbert F.
    Central tendency and variability / Herbert F. Weisberg.
        p.    cm.—(Sage university papers series. Quantitative
    applications in the social sciences; 07-083)
    Includes bibliographical references.
    ISBN 0-8039-4007-6 (pb)
    1. Social sciences—Methodology.   2. Social sciences—Statistical
    methods.   I. Title.   II. Series.
    H61.W4517   1992
    300'.1'5195—dc20                                                        91-34220


        99   00   01   11   10   9   8   7   6   5
Sage Production Editor: Astrid Virding

---

When citing a university paper, please use the proper form. Remember to cite the current Sage University Paper series title and include the paper number. One of the following formats can be adapted (depending on the style manual used):

(1) WEISBERG, H. F. (1992) Central Tendency and Variability. Sage University Paper Series on Quantitative Applications in the Social Sciences, 07-083. Newbury Park, CA: Sage.

*OR*

(2) Weisberg, H. F. (1992) *Central tendency and variability.* (Sage University Paper series on Quantitative Applications in the Social Sciences, series no. 07-083). Newbury Park, CA: Sage.

# CONTENTS

# SERIES EDITOR'S INTRODUCTION

When J. S. Mill declared that a *constant* was not susceptible to explanation, he meant that any scientific accounting starts from observing variation. Our phenomenon to be explained is a *variable,* perhaps related to other variables we have measured. Before examining those relationships, it is valuable to understand each of the variables, one at a time. In other words, the careful researcher first explores the univariate statistics. Indeed, it may even be that the most interesting hypotheses are actually univariate. Suppose Mary Black, a student of social stratification, has hypotheses about the "typical" income of families in River City, and about how "spread out" that income is. If so, she turns to measures of central tendency and variability, respectively.

Which measures should be chosen? Much depends on the level of measurement for the variable. Professor Weisberg, in lucid fashion, describes the three main levels—nominal, ordinal, and metric. Assuming the measure is metric (e.g., income in dollars), then student Black might consult the mean as her measure of "center." Is this the right choice? Perhaps not. What about the median? Or the mode? Or the midhinge from exploratory data analysis (EDA)? What about a trimmed mean? A geometric mean? The text at hand illuminates these and other possibilities. It also considers measures of center for nominal and ordinal data. Further, the presentation goes beyond offering an annotated menu of choices. Serious issues are tackled, such as "Should a mean be calculated on an ordinal variable?"

Measures of variability, or *spread,* also receive full treatment. The standard deviation (the square root of the variance) is the most widely used. But what does it tell us? How can we interpret whether the standard deviation is large or small? Weisberg suggests we might look at the coefficient of variation. Although measures for metric data are more developed, there is no neglect of ordinal measures (e.g., box plots and Leik's *D*) or nominal measures (e.g., the index of diversity and entropy).

After a thorough evaluation of these measures as descriptive statistics, their utility for inference is discussed. For example, suppose the mean is calculated from scores on a variable in a random sample, rather than in a whole population. What does this sample mean say about the true mean in the population? Understanding these rules of inference, simple enough where a mean is concerned, lays an essential foundation for more advanced statistical work.

Weisberg's monograph is comprehensive and exceptionally clear. In each chapter, the simpler material is at the beginning, the more difficult at the end. Thus, students at all levels can gain. For instance, the novice researcher, in trying to comprehend spread, might focus on mastering the standard deviation for metric data. By way of contrast, the advanced student or professor might wish to explore the more esoteric spread measures, such as Gini's mean difference, the coefficient of dispersion, or various EDA measures.

On this wide array of univariate topics, the reader will always encounter fine exposition. The monograph provides splendid preparation for taking the next step: bivariate and multivariate analysis. As such, it is a unique, logical precursor to several other monographs in our series.

—*Michael S. Lewis-Beck*
Series Editor

# CENTRAL TENDENCY AND VARIABILITY

**HERBERT F. WEISBERG**
*Ohio State University*

## 1. INTRODUCTION

"Variety is the spice of life," or, as the French say, "vive la différence." Statisticians agree—the study of variety and differences is what statistics is about. The statistical term for this is *variation*. Indeed, statistics is sometimes called the "science of variation." The concept of variation emphasizes that an interesting variable is one that varies, such that not every observation has the same score for the variable.

If the French seem captivated by "la différence," Americans seem more fascinated with "the typical." We want to know what typical people do and think, perhaps so that we can be sure that we ourselves are not unusual in our actions and attitudes. Statisticians also focus on measuring what is typical. The statistical term for this is *central tendency*, or, more simply, *center*. Variation emphasizes differences, whereas center emphasizes the typical.

This monograph explains how to measure the center and variation on a single variable, as a prelude to being able to study more complex interrelationships between variables. Pairing center and variation together in these pages emphasizes that neither is sufficient in itself—it is necessary to understand both.

### Measuring Center and Spread

There are actually several statistical questions that can be asked when analyzing a variable. The first is how the variable was measured. Variables can be measured with different numeric or nonnumeric properties, and this must be understood before statistical analysis is

AUTHOR'S NOTE: *I would like to thank William Jacoby, two anonymous reviewers, and Michael Lewis-Beck for their suggestions and comments on this monograph.*

begun. This concern is discussed in terms of *levels of measurement,* and is explained in Chapter 2.

The next statistical question about a variable is what kind of distribution its values have. The statistical summarization of a variable should include examining its distribution, especially graphically. Chapter 2 also shows some ways to examine distributions of variables.

The third statistical question about a variable is what a typical result is on it. That is what we shall call the *center* or *central tendency* of the variable. Averages are the most familiar example of central-tendency statistics. Measures of center also are termed *measures of location* or *representative values.* No single number can do justice to describing a variable on which different cases have different values, but a measure of center is a useful beginning point for summarizing variables. Chapter 3 explains several measures of center.

Thinking in terms of a typical value of a variable calls attention immediately to the fourth question: How typical is that typical value? That leads to measuring the *spread* of a variable in order to see how much the cases differ on the variable. This is also termed the *variation* on a variable, its *dispersion*, or its *scale.* Chapter 4 explains measures of spread.

A fifth question arises when a *sample* is studied but the researcher desires to describe a broader *population*: How do sample results generalize to the population? The applicability of the distinction between samples and populations to measuring center and spread will be presented in Chapter 5.

Once the amount of variation on a variable is measured, further statistical questions can be asked about it. Groups can be compared to find which vary most; variables can be compared to check how similar their values are; differences on a variable can be analyzed to see if they correspond to the differences on possible explanatory variables. Chapters 4 and 5 introduce these topics, showing ways in which the variation concept is used in practice.

Levels of measurement, distributions of variables, measures of center, and measures of spread are closely linked topics. A variable's level of measurement helps determine the appropriate ways of summarizing distributions and the appropriate measures of center and spread. Variation measures dispersion around the typical value of a variable, and generalizing from samples to populations is based on the variation of the variable. In these senses, Chapters 2 through 5 are tightly related.

The topics treated in this monograph are among the oldest in statistics. In addition to the classical ways of looking at them, there are also some newer ways. In particular, there has been a movement in applied statistics toward *exploratory data analysis*, usually abbreviated as EDA (Hartwig & Dearing, 1979). EDA emphasizes the virtue of becoming familiar with the data, rather than just computing one or two summary statistics. In part, the differences are stylistic; the EDA style has caught on with such new phrases as *measures of center* and *measures of spread*. Additionally, the EDA school has devised new measures of center and spread. This monograph introduces both the classical and EDA perspectives.

## Evaluating Measures of Center and Spread

In looking at measures of center and spread, we will find that there are several alternative measures. What considerations affect this choice between possible measures? The first criterion is that the measure be

1. appropriate for the measurement level of the variable.

This criterion is explained further in Chapter 2. However, there are often several measures that can be used at the same level, so choices must be made among these measures.

Another way of asking this is to ask what makes a good descriptive statistic. Many desirable properties for summary statistics have been proposed over the years. Yule and Kendall (1968: 103-104) state that an average should be

2. "rigidly defined" rather than just approximated,
3. based on all the observations,
4. simple and comprehensible,
5. calculated with ease,
6. expressed in algebraic terms, and
7. robust (little affected by fluctuations between samples).

Although none of these are absolutes, they are useful criteria for choosing and evaluating measures of center and spread.

Six additional desirable properties of such statistics are that they be

4

8. unique, rather than multivalued;
9. generalizable to two or more variables;
10. resistant to outliers (not overly affected by extreme cases);
11. not overly affected by combining categories;
12. defined even when a variable has open-ended categories; and
13. equal to actual data values, or at least in their metric.

As measures are described in Chapters 3 and 4, mention will be made when a statistic excels on any of these criteria or is weak on a criterion.

The distinction between populations and samples leads to three more formal criteria used to evaluate sample estimates: that they be

14. consistent for large samples,
15. unbiased for small samples, and
16. efficient when compared to other possible estimators.

These final criteria are too technical to consider until the end of this monograph.

No statistic is ideal on all 16 criteria, so it is necessary to decide which criteria are most important in actual data analysis situations. Furthermore, multiple measures often will prove useful for the same data, because each can be effective in portraying different aspects of the data.

## 2. LEVELS OF MEASUREMENT

A necessary beginning point in statistical analysis is to understand the measurement properties of the data (Jacoby, 1991: chap. 2; Weisberg, Krosnick, & Bowen, 1989: chap. 8). This is usually discussed in terms of each variable's *level of measurement.* Measurement itself can be defined as the process of assigning labels or values to observations. There are different types of assignment processes, resulting in variables with different mathematical properties.

Several levels of measurement are sometimes distinguished, but we shall find it useful to divide variables into three basic types: nominal, ordinal, and metric. Nominal variables consist of a series of unordered categories, as when categorizing a person's religion as Protestant, Catholic, Jewish, and so on. The variable is ordinal when there is an order to the categories, but no real unit of measurement. Metric variables are ones for which the categories are intrinsically numeric, like a person's age.[1]

We also shall distinguish a further measurement situation: dichotomous data. A dichotomous variable has only two categories, as when dealing with a person's gender. As we shall see, the usual level of measurement considerations do not apply fully for such variables.

The level of measurement of a variable is important because it limits the statistics that can appropriately be used on the variable. For example, values can be summed and averaged meaningfully only for strictly metric data. Nominal variables cannot be summed and averaged, and it is usually best not to sum and average ordinal variables. Similarly, the value of the middle case cannot be examined for nominal variables whose categories are unordered.

Metric analysis of ordinal variables should be precluded because they are nonnumeric. However, their ordered categories are presumed to reflect a continuous underlying concept, and that leads to a temptation to move ordinal variables up to the metric level. This tension will be returned to at several points in this monograph.

The level of measurement of a variable should be considered before performing statistical analysis on it, and even before collecting data. At the analysis stage, applying statistical techniques that require metric data to nominal variables would be fallacious. At the data-collection stage, metric versions of variables should be obtained, when possible, rather than nonmetric versions if metric-level analysis is planned. These implications can best be understood by explaining each basic level of measurement in greater detail.

**Nominal Scales**

The lowest level of measurement involves just categories, without order to these categories. Variables measured in this way are termed *nominal* variables. For example, the region of the country in which a person lives—either north, south, east, or west—is a nominal variable. These regions are just categories, with no particular order and no real numeric properties.

Numbers can be assigned to nominal variables, particularly to facilitate their analysis on the computer. Thus, regions might be coded as 1 for north, 2 for south, 3 for east, and 4 for west. However, these are just arbitrary numbers. We could as well code them 300 for north, 20 for south, 4,000 for east, and 1 for west, as there is no meaningful order to the categories.

Some nominal variables have numbered categories. If the numbers are assigned to label categories but the numerical order does not correspond to a property of the objects, then the variable is still nominal. Social security numbers are an example of numbers being used to label categories. There may be some system to how they are assigned, but they are not based on a single ordering principle. No one cares if their social security number is lower than another person's, because these numbers do not measure how much of an ordered property the objects have.[2]

As will be seen in Chapters 3 and 4, measures of center and spread have been developed for nominal variables based on the relative frequencies of observations in each category.

Before computing statistical summaries of variables, it is important to examine their distributions. One way to do so is to display the variable's *frequency distribution*. Each category is listed with its corresponding frequency—the number of observations falling into that category. The notation that will be used for the frequency of category $k$ will be $f_k$. The total number of cases will be denoted as $N$. Note that the sum of the frequencies of each separate category should equal the total number of observations. The symbol $\Sigma$ (the Greek letter *sigma*) is commonly used to represent a sum (with a subscript to show that the summation is over all possible different values of $k$—that is, over all categories). Using this notation (explained further in the appendix to this chapter),

$$N = \sum_k f_k.$$

Sometimes it is useful to show the proportion of cases falling into the particular category $k$. This proportion will be denoted as $p_k$. A proportion is the number of cases in the category divided by the total number of cases:

$$p_k = f_k / N.$$

Note that the proportions of the different categories on a variable will always add up to one. After all,

## TABLE 2.1
### Distribution of Crimes

| Crime | Frequency | Percentage |
|---|---|---|
| Homicide | 10,000 | 5 |
| Rape | 20,000 | 10 |
| Robbery | 40,000 | 20 |
| Assault | 60,000 | 30 |
| Burglary | 70,000 | 35 |
| Major | 30,000 | 15 |
| Minor | 40,000 | 20 |
| Total | 200,000 | 100 |

| Mode: | Five Major Categories Burglary | Burglaries Subdivided Assault |
|---|---|---|
| Variation ratio | .650 | .700 |
| Index of diversity | .735 | .795 |
| Index of qualitative variation | .919 | .954 |
| Entropy | 2.064 | 2.409 |
| Standardized entropy | .889 | .932 |

$$\sum_k p_k = \sum_k (f_k/N) = (1/N) \times \sum_k f_k = (1/N) \times N = 1.00.$$

Finally, the distribution on a variable can be represented by a *percentage distribution*, which shows the percentage of cases falling into each category. Percentages are just the proportions multiplied by 100. A percentage distribution should always sum to 100 percent.

As an example, consider the data in Table 2.1 showing the frequencies of different crimes in a city in which 200,000 crimes were reported in 1 year. The frequencies are shown in the second column and the corresponding percentages in the third column. According to these data, 35% of the crimes were burglaries, 30% assaults, 20% robberies, 10% rapes, and 5% homicides.

Frequency distributions can be portrayed effectively in graphs. The most common graph is the *bar chart*, as in Figure 2.1, section a. Each category is represented by a separate vertical bar whose height shows the category's frequency. A related diagram is a *pie chart*, as in Figure 2.1, section b. The unit circle is divided into a series of pieces standing for each category, with the size of a slice of the pie representing the proportion of cases falling into that category. Because the

8

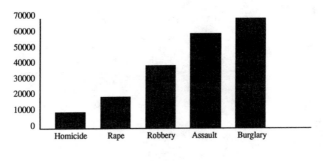

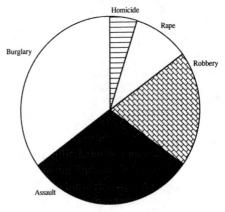

Figure 2.1. Section A. Bar Chart of Crime Reports
Section B. Pie Chart of Crime Reports

variable is nominal, the category order for these charts is arbitrary
and should not be overinterpreted.

**Ordinal Scales**

Some nonnumeric variables have an order to their categories. These
are called *ordinal variables.* For example, hospitals describe the condition of patients as "resting and comfortable," "stable," "guarded,"
or "critical." These categories are ordered but are not numeric. Note
especially that the intervals between these categories are not necessarily equal—there might be only a slight difference between describing the
patient's condition as "comfortable" versus "stable," in contrast to a

large difference between describing it as "guarded" versus "critical." Because the intervals between categories are not necessarily equal, this is only ordinal measurement.

Numbers are often assigned to ordinal data to facilitate storage and analysis on a computer, but that does not make them into true numeric data. The numbers assigned to ordinal variables can be termed *order numbers,* because only the order matters. As a result, adding them together or performing most other arithmetic operations on them would be inappropriate.

A common system for scoring ordinal variables is called *integer scoring:* the number 1 is assigned to the first category, the number 2 to the second, and so on. But even after integer scoring, the variable is ordinal because the categories are not necessarily equal steps apart on the continuum.

A prevalent type of ordinal data is ranked data. For example, it is customary to refer to the standings of sports teams in their league. These standings are numeric, like third or fourth in the league, but they are just order numbers. After all, the second-place team might have a winning percentage very close to that of the third-place team, but the third-place team might have a much higher winning percentage than the fourth-place team. Indeed, by examining the standings of the teams, we have converted numeric winning percentages into ordinal data.

Special measures of center and spread have been developed for ordinal data, and these will be presented in Chapters 3 and 4.

In dealing with ordinal data, it is important to understand the notion of a *percentile.* A percentile is a category of the variable below which a particular percentage of the observations fall. For example, the 50th percentile is the value below which 50% of the observations fall; the 25th percentile (also called the bottom *quartile*) is the value below which 25% of the observations fall; the 75th percentile (the top quartile) is the value below which 75% of the cases fall; and so on.

The distributions of ordinal variables are portrayed with the same type of frequency distributions and bar charts used for nominal variables.

## Metric Scales

A metric variable is one that has a unit of measurement, such as dollars or inches. Typically, numeric variables answer questions of how much or how many. For example, the price of objects is a metric variable, because it is an answer to the question "how much do the objects cost?"

Actually, there are two major types of metric variables—ratio and interval variables. The highest level of measurement is the *ratio scale*. Ratio variables are numeric, with a defined unit of measurement and a real zero point. For example, length is a ratio variable. It is intrinsically numeric, there is a defined unit of measurement (such as the inch), and it has a real zero point (zero inches).

The zero point is essential here. Because there is a zero point, *ratio statements* can be made, such as the statement that one person is twice as tall as another person. If it makes sense to consider one value twice as large as another, then the variable is ratio. Multiplication of a ratio variable by a constant does not destroy its ratio character, but addition of a constant to a ratio variable does. (For example, if an older sister is exactly twice as tall as a younger brother and both grow two inches, the ratio of their heights is no longer 2:1.) As a result, ratio variables can legitimately be transformed by multiplication, but not by addition.

Other numeric variables have a defined unit of measurement but lack a real zero point. These are termed *interval-level variables,* as their most important characteristic is the equal intervals between successive values. The usual example of an interval variable is temperature as measured on a Fahrenheit scale. Temperature is intrinsically numeric and there is a defined unit of measurement (the degree), but the zero point is not real because zero Fahrenheit does not mean the absence of temperature. (Temperature also can be measured on a ratio scale—the Kelvin scale, which is based on an absolute zero.) Because zero degrees Fahrenheit does not mean the absence of temperature, a 20-degree temperature is not twice as hot as a 10-degree temperature. (Adult shoe sizes are another example of an interval-level measurement.)

The units are fully meaningful for interval scales. There are equal intervals between, say, 20 and 21 degrees Fahrenheit and between 10 and 11 degrees. The amount of the property being measured, here heat, differs in each case by the same amount, so the intervals are real. Multiplication of an interval variable by a constant does not destroy its interval character, nor does addition of a constant injure its interval characteristics; as a result, interval variables are said to be transformable by linear rules.[3]

A further complication for metric data involves *grouping*. If a variable is continuous, then its values can take on any fractional value, such as a daily high temperature of 85.3235 degrees. Rather than give overly precise values, it is common to group the results into *classes* or *intervals* when preparing statistical presentations and analyses, as when saying that a daily high temperature was in the 80s.

Grouping the data draws attention to the *limits* of each interval. Say, for example, the classes are stated as 70-79, 80-89, and so on. How is a value such as 79.7 handled under such grouping? The *true limits* of an interval show its exact lower and upper limits. Thus, if values above 0.5 are routinely rounded up, then the true limits of the 80-89 interval are 79.5 and 89.5, so 79.7 is part of this interval. Note that this interval has a *width* of 10, because its true limits are 10 units apart. Its *midpoint* is 84.5 (the sum of the lower true limit and the upper true limit divided by 2).

If the analyst instead rounded all fractional values down to the next lowest integer (as is usually done with human ages), then the true limits of the 70-79 interval would be 70.0 and 80.0, so 79.7 would be part of this interval. The interval width is still 10, but the midpoint is 75.0. Either rounding system can be used, so long as the true limits are determined properly.

Graphs are effective for displaying distributions for metric variables. One type of graph is the *histogram*, as shown in the display of daily high temperatures in Figure 2.2, section a. Areas over categories (rather than heights of bars) represent relative frequencies. The total area under the histogram is 1.0, so the proportion of the area over a range of values shows the proportion of cases falling into that range. A related form of display is the *frequency polygon*, which is obtained by connecting the frequencies of each category with a line, as shown in Figure 2.2, section b. It is smoother than the histogram.

A more modern type of display is the *stem-and-leaf plot* (shown in Figure 2.2, section c), which lists the actual data values while showing the distribution's shape. The first digit is given on the left of the line; the values on the right show the last digits that occur. The top row shows that 65° occurs twice; the next row that 70°, 72°, and 73° occur once each. The 70° range has been divided into two categories, with separate rows for 70°-74° and 75°-79° (the same for the 80° range). Note from Figure 2.2 that it is common to use grouping for histograms, frequency polygons, and stem-and-leaf plots of metric variables.

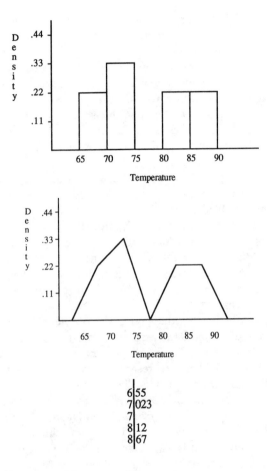

Figure 2.2. Section A. Histogram of Temperatures
Section B. Frequency Polygon of Temperatures
Section C. Stem-and-Leaf Plot of Temperatures


## Dichotomous Variables

Many social science variables are binary, such as whether or not a nation goes to war and whether a rat turns left or right in a maze. The usual level of measurement distinction matters less for measuring the center and spread of such dichotomous variables than for other data.

The dichotomous variable can be thought of as nominal, just two un-ordered categories. Or, the variable can be thought of as two ends of an ordinal variable. For example, whether or not a nation goes to war in a sense measures an underlying ordinal variable about the nation's propensity to engage in war.

Dichotomous variables are also often treated as metric by assigning the value of 1 to one category (usually to mark the presence of some attribute) and 0 to the other category (to mark its absence). This is called *dummy-variable* scoring. As an example, whether or not the country went to war can be scored 1/0, 1 for the country going to war and 0 for it not going to war. This scoring may seem arbitrary, but there is no loss of generality.

The distribution for a dichotomous variable can be shown by giving the likelihood of a "success" for a single observation. This is the propor-tion of 1 scores (as opposed to 0 scores). This proportion, or probability, is $f_1$ (the frequency of 1s) divided by the total number of cases:

$$p = f_1/N = 1 - (f_0/N).$$

## Categorization Rules

There are two constraints on categorizations that hold at every mea-surement level: A proper categorization should be *mutually exclusive* and *exhaustive*. Requiring categories to be mutually exclusive means that each case should fall into only one category. Requiring categories to be exhaustive means that each case should fit into some category; no case can be left out of the classification. A variable consisting of catego-ries that are not mutually exclusive or exhaustive should be revised to make its categorization more consistent prior to statistical analysis.

Making a categorization exhaustive often requires including one or more categories to represent *missing data*. For example, when collect-ing data on the illness of people in hospital beds, some hospitals might not provide full information. Missing data categories are gener-ally omitted from statistical analysis when they are irrelevant.[4]

## Appendix: Summation Notation

In several places in the text it is necessary to examine summations of a series of values. The usual convention is to represent the separate values with a letter to denote the variable (such as $X$) and a subscript to show the case number: 1 for the first case, 2 for the second, and so on, up to $N$, where $N$ is the total number of cases. The summation of the $X$ values is denoted by using a capital Greek letter sigma ($\Sigma$). The full notation to represent the sum of all the $X$s, from $X_1$ through $X_N$, is

$$\sum_{i=1}^{N} X_i = X_1 + X_2 + \ldots + X_N.$$

This is read as "the summation of $X$-sub-$i$, from $i$ to 1 to $N$." It is often written in an abbreviated style as $\Sigma_i X_i$, or even more simply as $\Sigma X$.

Some rules about summations must be understood in order to follow the derivations in the text. For example, say that each value of $X$ is multiplied separately by the same constant $c$ ($c$ could be the number 2 or any other number). Summing a series of numbers that have been multiplied by the same constant is the same as multiplying the sum of the numbers by that constant:

$$\sum c X_i = c X_1 + c X_2 + \ldots + c X_N = c(X_1 + X_2 + \ldots + X_N) = c \times \sum X_i.$$

The summation of a constant $N$ times is the same as $N$ times that constant:

$$\sum_{i=1}^{N} c = c + c + \ldots + c = N \times c.$$

Summing a series of numbers that have a constant subtracted from them is the same as subtracting $N$ times that constant from the sum of the numbers:

$$\sum (X_i - c) = X_1 - c + X_2 - c + \ldots + X_N - c = \sum X_i - (N \times c).$$

In some proofs in the text, variables are multiplied by their means or the mean is subtracted from each value of the variable. In these equations, the mean can be treated as the constant following the rules above. Thus, summing the values of $X$ multiplied by their mean, $\overline{X}$ (called "$X$-bar"), is the same as multiplying the sum of the original numbers by the mean:

$$\sum \overline{X}X_i = \overline{X}X_1 + \overline{X}X_2 + \ldots + \overline{X}X_N = \overline{X}\,(X_1 + X_2 + \ldots + X_N) = \overline{X}\sum X_i\,.$$

Similarly, summing the difference between the values of $X$ and their mean is the same as subtracting $N$ times the mean from the sum of the original numbers:

$$\sum (X_i - \overline{X}) = X_1 - \overline{X} + X_2 - \overline{X} + \ldots + X_N - \overline{X} = \sum X_i - (N \times \overline{X})\,.$$

It is also sometimes necessary to work with a sum of squared values. The sum of squares of the values of $X$ is denoted as

$$\sum_{i=1}^{N} X_i^2 = X_1^2 + X_2^2 + \ldots + X_N^2\,.$$

This is not equivalent to squaring the sum of the variable $X$:

$$\left(\sum_{i=1}^{N} X_i\right)^2 = (X_1 + X_2 + \ldots + X_N)^2 = X_1^2 + 2X_1X_2 + X_2^2 + \ldots \neq \sum_{i=1}^{N} X_i^2\,.$$

## 3. MEASURES OF CENTER

Measures of center summarize the typical value of a variable. They are often thought of as averages, though the familiar average is not always the most appropriate way to summarize *center*. There are three major statistics that are used to gauge different aspects of what is typical for a variable: the *mode*, which must be used on nominal data; the *median*, which is appropriate for ordinal data; and the *mean*, which is used extensively on metric data. These three central-tendency measures will be presented in detail in this chapter, along with some other measures that are employed in specific measurement circumstances. The choice of the proper statistic for particular measurement situations will be emphasized, but it should be remembered that it can be useful to employ multiple measures to summarize different aspects of data.

### Mode

The simplest summary of a variable is to indicate which category is the most common. The *mode* measures a variable's center by pointing to the most typical category.

*The Mode for Nominal Data.* If the data are strictly nominal, then the only possible measure of center is assessing which category occurs most often:

Mode = category occurring with greatest frequency.

The mode can also be determined for ordinal and metric data, but it is especially valuable for nominal data. Note that the mode is actually a category, not the frequency of that category.

As an example, say we are dealing with crime statistics during the past year for one city. If there were 10,000 reported cases of homicide, 20,000 rapes, 40,000 robberies, 60,000 assaults, and 70,000 burglaries (see Table 2.1), then burglary would be the mode because more reported crimes were burglaries than any other crime.

The mode is an important statistic for nominal data because it is impossible to take averages to measure the center of a nominal variable. The average crime cannot be determined in Table 2.1, for example, because the categories are not numeric. Even if numbers were assigned to the categories (like 1 for homicide, 2 for rape, 3 for robbery, 4 for assault, and 5 for burglary), finding an average crime of 3.80 would be meaningless because the numbers are arbitrary. Note too that it would not make sense to average the percentages in the categories. Averaging 5%, 10%, 20%, 30%, and 35% to get 20% as the rate of the average crime is not meaningful, because any distribution of cases across five categories would give an average rate of 20% of the cases per crime. Averages only work when the variable has a unit of measurement.

The mode is a measure of central tendency in the sense of showing what the typical category is on a variable. The "average" or the "typical" American is often described as Protestant because more U.S. residents are Protestant than any other single religion. This is a case of using the mode as the measure of center.

Another interpretation of the mode is that it provides the "best guess" as to the category a case has on the variable, *if* the goal is to be accurate as often as possible. That is, no other guess of a category for a random case would be correct as often as the mode is. Using the example in Table 2.1, say a person guessed what the crime was in a particular crime report. Because more burglaries were reported than any other crimes, the "best guess" is that a particular crime would be a burglary. That guess would not always be correct, but it would be correct 35% of the time, a higher success rate than would be achieved from any other guess.

The main advantage of the mode as a statistic is that it is easy to obtain and to interpret. Consequently, the mode is usually simple to communicate and explain to people.

There are four problems involved in dealing with the mode on non-numeric data. First, it may not be very descriptive of the data, because the most common category still may not occur very often. That burglary is the most common crime in a community says little, unless the prevalence of that crime also is indicated. By itself, the mode provides little information.

The second problem with the mode is that it may not be unique. For example, two categories may be equally likely and more common than any other category. A variable with such a distribution is termed *bimodal*. Indeed, several categories may be equally likely and may occur more often than any remaining category, in which case the variable is *multimodal*. In the most extreme case, if each category occurred with the same frequency, there would be no mode for the variable.

A third problem is that the mode can be overly affected by sampling variation. Imagine taking several samples and measuring a variable that has a bimodal distribution with population modes $X_1$ and $X_2$. Many samples would have $X_1$ as their mode, while many other samples would have $X_2$ as their mode. Thus, the mode would fluctuate considerably from sample to sample.

The fourth problem is that the mode is very sensitive to how categories are combined. The classification scheme should be at the same level of generality for all categories, rather than more general for some categories than others. The mode can, in fact, be manipulated by making the level of generality of different categories unequal. For example, Table 2.1 divides the 70,000 burglary cases into 40,000 cases of minor theft and 30,000 cases of major theft. Should these two categories be used instead of the one, the mode is no longer burglary. It is now assault because there are more assault cases than any other single category of crime. When reading a statistical analysis that reports a mode, always be sure to examine the categories to make sure that the modal category was not manipulated by using categories at different levels of generality.

These problems notwithstanding, the mode is commonly used to measure the center for nominal data because it fits exactly the assumptions appropriate for that level of measurement.

*The Mode for Metric Data.* Although the mode is particularly important for nominal data, the mode also can be used on other variables, even numeric data. Obtaining the mode for numeric data is just a matter of seeing which value occurs most frequently. If the variable is denoted as $X$, then

$$X_{mode} = X \text{ value occurring with greatest frequency.}$$

For example, Table 3.1, section a, reports hypothetical data on the number of wars in which seven nations have participated. In this case, the mode is 1 because that value occurs most often.

Occasionally confusion develops as to what the modal value is for metric data. For one thing, the mode is an actual value, not the frequency of occurrence. With the values in Table 3.1, the value of 1 occurs twice, but the mode is 1 rather than 2. Along the same line, the mode is not the largest value (50), it is the value that occurs most frequently: 1.

To shift to a real example, Table 3.2, section a, lists how often each American president from Hoover to Reagan was elected president. Section b displays the same data as a frequency distribution. The first column gives the number of times a president was elected, and the second column shows how many presidents during this time period were elected that number of times. The modal value for such a display is the category with the highest frequency in the frequency column. The most frequently occurring value occurs five times, and that corresponds to electing a president to office once, so the mode is 1.

*The Mode for Grouped Metric Data.* Grouping is a common strategy for dealing with numeric variables. Rather than listing every possible value for the variable separately, the variable is divided into a set of classes that cover a range of values. The mode then shows which class occurs most often:

$$\text{Mode} = \text{class occurring with greatest frequency.}$$

The example to be used in this section involves daily high temperatures (see Figure 2.2). The exact high temperatures (like 82°) could be recorded, or the data could be grouped by counting how many days had high temperatures in the 70s, in the 80s, and so on.

Some further complications arise when working with grouped metric data. For one thing, the mode is strongly affected by the number

TABLE 3.1
Twentieth-Century Wars (hypothetical data)

| Section A. Number of Wars, by Nation | | Section B. Frequency Distribution of Wars | | |
|---|---|---|---|---|
| Nation | Number of Wars | Number of Wars | Frequency | Percentage |
| Algeria | 1 | 1 | 2 | 28.6 |
| Australia | 2 | 2 | 1 | 14.3 |
| England | 3 | 3 | 1 | 14.3 |
| Switzerland | 50 | 4 | 1 | 14.3 |
| Tanzania | 1 | 9 | 1 | 14.3 |
| Togo | 9 | 50 | 1 | 14.3 |
| Turkey | 4 | | | |
| Number of cases | 7 | | 7 | 100.1 |

| Center | | Spread | Population | Sample |
|---|---|---|---|---|
| Mode | 1 | Mean deviation | 11.43 | |
| Median | 3 | Variance | 273.14 | 318.67 |
| Mean | 10 | Standard deviation | 16.53 | 17.85 |
| | | Coefficient of variation | 1.65 | 1.78 |
| Midextreme | 25.5 | Gini's mean difference | 15.71 | |
| Upper quartile | 9 (6.5)* | | | |
| Bottom quartile | 1 (2.5) | Range | 49 | |
| Midhinge | 5 (4.5) | Interquartile range | 8 (4) | |
| Trimean | 4 (3.75) | Quartile deviation | 4 (2) | |
| Biweight | 8.03 | Coefficient of quartile variation | .80 (.44) | |
| | | MAD | 2 | |
| | | AD | 8.43 | |
| | | Coefficient of dispersion | 2.81 | |
| | | Leik's $D$ | .63 | |
| | | Variation ratio | .71 | |
| | | Index of diverstiy | .82 | |
| | | Index of qualitative variation | .98 | |
| | | Entropy | 2.52 | |
| | | Standardized entropy | .98 | |

of class intervals and their sizes. Say we were dealing with high temperatures for a city, each rounded to a whole number (see Table 3.3). Consider, for example, the high temperatures 65°, 65°, 70°, 72°, 73°, 81°, 82°, 86°, and 87°. The mode of those separate temperatures is 65° (section a), but the mode is the 70°-74° range if they are grouped

TABLE 3.2
U.S. Presidents, 1928-1984

| Section A | | Section B | | |
|---|---|---|---|---|
| President | # Times Elected | # Times Elected | Frequency | Percentage |
| Hoover | 1 | 0 | 1 | 10 |
| F. D. Roosevelt | 4 | 1 | 5 | 50 |
| Truman | 1 | 2 | 3 | 30 |
| Eisenhower | 2 | 3 | 0 | 0 |
| Kennedy | 1 | 4 | 1 | 10 |
| Johnson | 1 | | | |
| Nixon | 2 | Total | 10 | 100 |
| Ford | 0 | | | |
| Carter | 1 | | | |
| Reagan | 2 | | | |
| Number of cases: | 10 | | | |

| Center | | Spread | Population | Sample |
|---|---|---|---|---|
| Mode | 1 | Mean deviation | .80 | |
| Rough median | 1 | Variance | 1.05 | 1.17 |
| Exact median | 1.3 | Standard deviation | 1.02 | 1.08 |
| Mean | 1.5 | Coefficient of variation | .68 | .72 |
| | | Gini's mean difference | 1.13 | |
| Midextreme | 2 | | | |
| Upper quartile | 2 | Range | 4 | |
| Bottom quartile | 1 | Interquartile range | 1 | |
| Midhinge | 1.50 | Quartile deviation | 1 | |
| Trimean | 1.25 | Coefficient of | | |
| Biweight | 1.505 | quartile variation | .33 | |
| | | MAD | .50 | |
| | | AD | .70 | |
| | | Coefficient of dispersion | .70 | |
| | | Leik's $D$ | .35 | |
| | | Variation ratio | .50 | |
| | | Index of diverstiy | .64 | |
| | | Index of qualitative | | |
| | | variation | .85 | |
| | | Entropy | 1.68 | |
| | | Standardized entropy | .84 | |

into intervals of five degrees (section b), and the 80°-89° range if they are grouped into intervals of 10 degrees (section c). The mode can be very unsteady when data values are grouped together.

TABLE 3.3
Daily High Temperatures

| Section A | | Section B | |
| --- | --- | --- | --- |
| Temperature | Frequency | Temperature | Frequency |
| 65° | 2 | 65°-69° | 2 |
| 70° | 1 | 70°-74° | 3 |
| 72° | 1 | 75°-79° | 0 |
| 73° | 1 | 80°-84° | 2 |
| 81° | 1 | 85°-89° | 2 |
| 82° | 1 | | |
| 86° | 1 | Number of cases | 9 |
| 87° | 1 | | |
| | | Mode | 70°-74° |
| Number of cases | 9 | Crude mode | 72° |
| | | Refined mode | 70.75° |
| Mode | 65° | | |

| Section C | |
| --- | --- |
| Temperature | Frequency |
| 65°-69° | 2 |
| 70°-79° | 3 |
| 80°-89° | 4 |
| Number of cases | 9 |
| Mode | 80°-89° |
| Crude mode | 84.5° |
| Refined mode | 81.5° |

When dealing with grouped numeric data, a distinction is made between the *crude mode* and the *refined mode*. The crude mode is just the midpoint of the interval of the most frequent category. That is,

Crude Mode = midpoint of most frequent interval.

Using the classes of width 10° in Table 3.3, section c, the most frequently occurring category is 80°-89°, so the crude mode would be 84.5°. By contrast, the refined mode adjusts the modal value according to the relative frequencies of the adjacent intervals. It pulls the modal value toward the adjacent interval that has the greater frequency. Let $L$ be the true lower limit of the modal interval, let $w$ be the width of the class interval, let $f_{mo}$ be the frequency of the modal interval, let $f_b$ be the frequency of the interval *below* the modal interval, and let $f_a$ be the frequency of the interval *above* the modal interval. The formula for the refined mode is then

$$\text{Refined Mode} = L + \frac{w\,(f_{mo} - f_b)}{(f_{mo} - f_b) + (f_{mo} - f_a)}$$

In Table 3.3, section c, the width of the class interval is 10°, the modal interval is 80°-89°, the true lower limit of that interval is 79.5°, the frequency of the modal interval is 4, the frequency of the next lower interval (70°-79°) is 3, and the frequency of the next higher interval (90°-99°) is 0. Therefore, the refined mode is

$$79.5° + \frac{10° \times (4-3)}{(4-3) + (4-0)} = 79.5° + \frac{10°}{1+4} = 79.5° + \frac{10°}{5}$$

$$= 79.5° + 2° = 81.5°.$$

The refined mode is on the low side of the 80°-89° interval to reflect the fact that more days had temperatures just below that than just above it.

## Median

When the categories of a variable are ordered, a measure of center should take that order into account. The *median* does so by finding the value of the variable corresponding to the middle case. It is a positional measure, showing the category for the central observation.

*The Median for Ordinal Data.* The usual way to summarize the typical value for an ordinal variable is to determine the category in which the "middle" observation falls:

Median = category of the middle case.

The median is a *location* or *positional* or *order* measure, in that it locates the position of the typical value along the variable's ordering. Remember that the median computed on ordinal data is not numeric because ordinal variables are not numeric.

As an example, say that seven people rated a company's service record, three rating its performance as "excellent," and one each rating it "very good," "good," "fair," and "poor." The middle person rated the company's service as "very good," so that is the median on this ordinal scale.

The median is important for ordinal data partly because of the limitations of other measures for such data. The mode can be obtained for ordinal data, but it does not take into account the category order, which is what makes the variable more than just a nominal classification. Furthermore, the mode can be unrepresentative for an ordinal variable. Say that three valedictorians in a graduating class share the top class rank because they all had perfect grade-point averages, and the remaining 97 students each fell in a separate category but with very low grade-point averages. The mode in this example would correspond to the valedictorians, even though they are extremely unrepresentative of the class as a whole.

At the same time, it would not be meaningful to take averages on ordinal data because category numbers are arbitrary. For example, say we asked people to rate the quality of service provided by a company, and used integer scoring to assign numbers to the categories (1 for excellent, 2 for very good, and so on). Finding that the average rating of the service delivery is 2.43 would not be very meaningful, because the units between the five verbal labels are not necessarily equal. Having issued that warning, it is necessary to admit that it is becoming more common to compute averages on ordinal variables. Many researchers are finding that a useful way to summarize their data, even if doing so increases the chances of drawing fallacious conclusions.

There are two main advantages of the median. First, it is relatively easy to obtain. Second, it is based on the whole distribution rather than just a small part of the distribution the way the mode is.

There are two complications to consider in dealing with the median. The first is that a category is middle only with respect to some ordering, so it is essential to think in terms of that ordering when determining the median. Decide what the underlying ordered property is, and then order the cases according to that property before computing the median. The categories *must* be properly ordered before determining the median. For example, say that seven people were asked to rate a company's service record, and the order in which the responses were recorded was "poor," "excellent," "excellent," "fair," "excellent," "very good," and "good." The middle rating is "fair," but that really is not the median category. The ratings should first be put into the proper evaluative order: excellent, excellent, excellent, very good,

good, fair, and poor. The middle rating of the company's service is "very good," so that is the median category.

The second complication involves determining the middle case. *Middle* is well defined when the number of cases is odd, but not when it is even. Imagine a small classroom in which there is a row with only three students in it. The middle student is clearly the second student—and that is the same student whether counting from the left to the right or counting from the right to the left. However, what if there are four students in the row? Who is the middle student? In a sense, the second and third students are together the middle. In another sense, there is no middle. The middle position is between the second and third students. The usual way of thinking about the median for an even number of cases is that it is halfway between the two middle cases.

There is a formula for determining which ordered case is the middle one. If there are $N$ observations, then the middle case is the $(N + 1)/2$th case. That is

$$\text{Median} = \text{category of the } (N + 1)/2 \text{th case.}$$

Thus, with three cases, $N$ is 3, and the median is the category of the $(3 + 1)/2 = 4/2 = 2$nd case. With four cases, $N$ is 4, and the median is the category of the $(4 + 1)/2 = 5/2 = 2.5$th case: halfway between the second and third cases.

*The Median for Metric Data.* Although the median is most important for ordinal data, it is also sometimes used for metric variables. For metric data, the median indicates the value of the variable (which we label $X$) for the middle case. As with ordinal data, it is essential that the variable be properly ordered before computing the median. If there are $N$ ordered observations, then the middle is the $(N + 1)/2$th observation. So,

$$X_{\text{median}} = \text{value of } X \text{ for the } (N + 1)/2 \text{th ordered case, for odd } N,$$

and

$$= \text{average of } N/2 \text{th and } [(N/2) + 1] \text{th ordered case, for even } N.$$

By the way, $(N + 1)/2$ is *not* the median for odd $N$; it is the *location* of the median in the ordered set of values.

As an example, we return to the numbers of wars in which different countries participated (Table 3.1, section a). With the countries listed in alphabetical order, the number of wars are 1, 2, 3, 50, 1, 9, and 4. This makes it seem like the middle value is 50, but it is not. The variable is the number of wars in which the country has fought, and the values must be put into the proper order (1, 1, 2, 3, 4, 9, and 50) before obtaining the median. When ordered properly, the median is seen to be 3 wars.

With numeric data for an even number of cases, the median is defined as halfway between the values for the two center cases. For example, say we had data on participation in wars for only four countries, and the number of wars they had been in were 1, 3, 4, and 50, respectively. Would the middle case be the second with 3 wars, or the third with 4 wars, or what? The median is 3.5, halfway between the 3 and the 4, even though no country could be in 3.5 wars.

There are two further advantages of the median for numeric data. First, it is not affected by extreme values on the variable. Some measures of center are considerably deflected by atypical extreme cases (like the 50 value in the above example), but the median is not. It nicely captures where the middle of the distribution is, and that is not affected by unusual "outliers." As a result, the median is considered a *resistant* statistic.

A second special advantage of the median is that it sometimes can be computed even when a distribution is open-ended at the extremes. Consider, for example, the problem of determining the typical age of death of various high school graduating classes. Say that one graduating class had only 5 graduates—one who died young at age 30, a second who lasted until age 67, a third who died at 80, and two more who are still alive and are both 87 years old. The median age of death for this graduating class is clearly 80, and that can be determined without waiting to see how long the two remaining members survive. Neither the mode nor the average can yet be determined in this example, only the median. Note also in this example that the median is not deflected by the outlier, the one person who died unusually young.

Because of these two special advantages, the median is sometimes useful even for metric data. The median should be considered as the measure of center when there are extreme outliers or when the process being observed is open-ended at an extreme.

The median actually has a special optimal property for metric data. Describing this property requires introducing a new concept: the *deviation* of an observation from the measure of center. Some notation is useful here. Label the variable being studied $X$. Then let $X_i$ be the observation for the $i$th case. Let $X_c$ be the measure of center. The deviation $d_i$ for the $i$th case then is $d_i = X_i - X_c$. This deviation shows how much the $i$th observation's value on the variable differs from the measure of center. Next, define the *absolute deviation* as the unsigned magnitude of that deviation: $|d_i| = |X_i - X_c|$.

The special property of the median is that the sum of these absolute deviations around the median is minimal. In other words, the sum of absolute deviations computed from the median is smaller than the sum of absolute deviations computed from any other possible measure of center. That is, $\Sigma|d_i| = \Sigma|X_i - X_c|$ is minimized when $X_c$ is the median (Blalock, 1972: 60).

As a result of this property, the median is the value that is closest to all the other scores on a variable. (An implication of this property is that the average absolute deviation is minimal when taken from the median, a result that will be used in the next chapter.) This special property gives the median a "best guess interpretation." The median is the best guess of a case's score *if* the goal is to minimize the absolute deviation; if the sign of the error in guessing does not matter but its magnitude does, then the median is the best guess as to a case's score on the variable.

*The Median for Grouped Metric Data.* A problem occurs with the median for grouped metric data in determining the middle case when there are several cases sharing that value. If the prices of five items at a hardware store were $2, $4, $4, $7, and $30, then is the first 4 or the second 4 the middle value? At first, that might seem like a senseless question, because 4 is 4 (is 4). But say that these prices have been rounded to the nearest dollar. In other words, $4 stands for a cost of $3.50 to $4.49. If the prices are $2, $4, $4, $7, and $30, then there is a real sense in which the middle case is the higher of the two $4 items. We do not know the exact values of the items, but we could assume that any value in that range ($3.50 to $4.49) is equally likely, so the higher item is likely to be closer to $4.49 than to $3.50. Another way of thinking about this is that we are wondering how "deep" into that category (or class) the middle value is. Because there are more cases above $4 than below $4, we have to go well into the $4 category to get to the middle case, so the middle value will be on the high side of $4.

In dealing with the median for such data, a distinction is made between the *rough median* and the *exact median*. The rough median is just the value corresponding to the middle case:

Rough Median = midpoint of class containing middle case.

The formula to obtain the exact median in this situation is

$$\text{Exact Median} = L + \frac{w\,(0.5N - C)}{f_{\text{median}}}$$

where $L$ is the true lower limit of the class containing the 50th percentile, $C$ is the cumulative frequency below the class containing the 50th percentile, $f_{\text{median}}$ is the frequency of the class containing the 50th percentile, and $w$ is the width of the interval containing the 50th percentile. This can be thought of as treating the cases in the median class as uniformly distributed through that interval. In the above example, the rough median is $4, but the exact median is $4.25. Usually the rough median of a set of numbers is all that is required, but sometimes the exact median is of interest.

Looking back at the earlier example of the numbers of times various presidents were elected to the office, if we looked at the 1928-1984 period (Table 3.2, section a), the values would be 1, 4, 1, 2, 1, 1, 2, 0, 1, and 2. Put in the proper order (section b), these values would read: 0, 1, 1, 1, 1, 1, 2, 2, 2, 4. The rough median would be 1, and the exact median would be 1.3. The exact median is on the high end of the 1 range (0.5 to 1.4999), because we have to go through most of the 1 cases to get up to the middle case.

## Mean

Generally the most effective way of summarizing the center of metric data is to average the values on the variable. This statistic is known technically as the *mean*. It is a measure of the central tendency for variables that are fully numeric.

*The Mean for Metric Data.* The mode and median can be obtained for metric data, but they do not take full advantage of the numeric information inherent in the data. The mean fully considers that metric information.

The most common way to determine the typical value for a numeric variable is to compute the arithmetic average of its values. This is called the *mean* (or *arithmetic mean*) of the variable. To obtain the average, sum all the values and divide by the number of cases.

Although it is easy to calculate the mean from the above description, it is important to become familiar with the notation that will be used for other statistical calculations. The notation for the mean of a variable $X$ is $\overline{X}$, called "X-bar." The formula for the mean is then

$$\overline{X} = \frac{\sum_{i=1}^{N} X_i}{N} = \frac{X_1 + X_2 + \ldots + X_N}{N}.$$

In this formula, the letter $N$ stands for the number of cases. The letter $i$ stands for the case number (the first case, the second case, etc.), and $X_i$ is the $i$th case's value on the variable $X$. The Greek letter $\Sigma$ (capital sigma) stands for "summation." As explained in the appendix to Chapter 2, the notation below and above the sigma is read as "the summation over $i$, from $i$ equals 1 to $N$" and is a way of saying that we are summing all values of $X_i$. After obtaining the sum of the $X$s, just divide by $N$ to get the mean, $\overline{X}$.

As an example, Table 3.1, section a, gives hypothetical values for the numbers of wars in which seven nations participated in the 20th century. To obtain the mean of the numbers, first add the values together $(1 + 2 + 3 + 50 + 1 + 9 + 4 = 70)$. Then divide by the number of cases (7 nations) to obtain the mean of 10 $(= 70/7)$. Similarly, to obtain the mean number of times the presidents from Hoover to Reagan were elected (Table 3.2, section a), sum the separate numbers (which gives a sum of 15), and divide by the number of presidents (10); the resulting mean is 1.5 $(= 15/10)$.

The mean has several properties that make it unique and useful. In presenting them, it is necessary to use the notation for deviations from the mean. If the mean for variable $X$ is denoted as $\overline{X}$, then the deviation of observation $i$s score on $X$ from the mean is denoted as $d_i = X_i - \overline{X}$. This deviation shows how far off each value is from the mean.

The first property of importance for the mean is that *the total sum of deviations around the mean is always zero.* The proof is direct. Recall that $\Sigma X_i/N = \overline{X}$; multiplying both sides by $N$ shows that $\Sigma X_i = N\overline{X}$. Also, adding the mean to itself $N$ times is the same as multiplying it by $N$, so $\Sigma \overline{X} = N\overline{X}$. Thus

$$\sum (X_i - \overline{X}) = \sum X_i - \sum \overline{X} = N\overline{X} - \sum \overline{X} = N\overline{X} - N\overline{X} = 0.$$

The mean is unique in that sense: the sum total of deviations around any other value would be higher. That the sum of deviations around the mean is zero implies also that the average signed deviation around the mean is zero.

This property leads to an interpretation of the mean as a "best guess" statistic. Say we sought to guess the value of a particular score, such that the sum of the signed errors in guessing (or the average signed error in guessing) is minimized. Because the sum of the signed deviations from the mean is zero, the mean is the best guess of a score on the variable *if* the goal is to minimize the sum (or average) of signed errors.

The second important property of the mean is that *the sum of negative deviations from the mean exactly equals the sum of positive deviations*. This must be the case because the grand total of the deviations is zero, so negative deviations are balanced by positive deviations. This property leads to a special interpretation of the mean as a balance point (or fulcrum) for the distribution of values. It is a balance point in the sense that negative deviations are exactly balanced by positive deviations. To whatever extent some values are below the mean, they are offset by some other values that are equally above that mean.

The third property of the mean involves squared deviations: *The sum of the squared deviations around the mean is smaller than the sum of the squared deviations around any other value*. To prove this, consider the deviation of the observation $X_i$ from an arbitrary value, $X_0$. The deviation, $X_i - X_0$, is not changed if the same value (say $\overline{X}$), is added to it and subtracted from it:

$$X_i - X_0 = (X_i - \overline{X}) + (\overline{X} - X_0).$$

Squaring both sides of this identity gives

$$(X_i - X_0)^2 = (X_i - \overline{X})^2 + 2(\overline{X} - X_0)(X_i - \overline{X}) + (\overline{X} - X_0)^2.$$

Next, sum both sides over the $N$ observations to get the sum of squared deviations from the arbitrary value $X_0$, which is to be minimized:

$$\sum (X_i - X_0)^2 = \sum (X_i - \overline{X})^2 + \sum 2(\overline{X} - X_0)(X_i - \overline{X}) + \sum (\overline{X} - X_0)^2.$$

The three terms on the right-hand side of this equation must now each be examined separately. The first term is the sum of squared deviations from the mean. The second term is zero, because $\Sigma 2(\overline{X} - X_0)(X_i - \overline{X}) = 2(\overline{X} - X_0)\Sigma(X_i - \overline{X}) = 2(\overline{X} - X_0) \times 0 = 0$, because the sum of deviations from the mean is zero. The third term is just $N(\overline{X} - X_0)^2$ because $(\overline{X} - X_0)^2$ is a constant that is being added to itself $N$ times. A squared term cannot be negative, so this third term is minimized when $X_0 = \overline{X}$, in which case the term equals zero. As a result, the sum of squared deviations around a fixed arbitrary value $X_0$ is minimized when that value is the mean, $\overline{X}$. As shall be seen in the next chapter, this *least-squares* property is important in measuring the spread of a metric variable.

In addition to the properties just described, there are two further advantages of the mean as a measure of center. First, it is more stable than other possible measures—over repeated samples, the mean would have less variation than would other measures of center. Second, other important statistics (especially variance and covariance) are based on deviations from the mean. These advantages will become more evident in later chapters.

Three problems with the mean should also be mentioned. First, it can have fractional values, even when the variable itself can sensibly take on only integer values. This problem is evident in Table 3.2, where the mean number of times these presidents were elected to office is 1.5, a value that cannot occur. This actually is a problem for how fractional values of the mean should be interpreted, rather than a limitation of the mean itself.

A second problem with the mean is that it cannot be computed when extreme categories of a variable are open-ended. For example, the mean income would be indeterminate if one category included incomes of $1 million or more.

A final problem with the mean is that it is strongly affected by extreme cases. Recall the earlier example (Table 3.1) involving the number of wars in which seven nations had participated. The mode was 1 and the median 3, but the mean was much larger: 10 wars. The mean here is much larger than the other central-tendency measures because the mean is affected by the 50 case, whereas the mode and median are not sensitive to it. The mode and median tend to be around where the bulk of the values are, but the mean can be drawn away toward the extreme case. Because the mean is affected by atypical outliers, it is considered *nonresistant* in contrast to more resistant measures of center such as the median.

*The Mean for Grouped Metric Data.* A special version of the mean formula can be used when the data are grouped. When several cases have the same value, the summation in the numerator can be simplified. Instead of summing the separate values, each value is multiplied by its frequency and these products are added together. This sum is then divided by the number of cases as before to get the mean. The grouped mean formula is

$$\overline{X} = \sum (X_i f_i)/N = \sum (X_i f_i)/\sum f_i,$$

where $f_i$ is the frequency of category $i$.

As an example, consider again the data in Table 3.2 on the numbers of times the ten presidents from Hoover to Reagan were elected to office. We can summarize the data as one president being elected zero times, five being elected once, three being elected twice, and one being elected four times. The original computation of the mean added these values together, but it would be equivalent to multiply 1 times 0 (= 0), multiply 5 times 1 (= 5), multiply 3 times 2 (= 6), and multiply 1 times 4 (= 4), and then sum the products (0 + 5 + 6 + 4 = 15). Dividing by the number of cases, 10, gives the mean of 1.5. Thus the group mean formula gives the same result as the usual formula or the mean; it is just an easier formula when some values occur repeatedly.

When a continuous variable is grouped into classes of interval width greater than one, the mean formula can be used with a minor adjustment—the midpoint of the true class limits defined in Chapter 2 should be used to represent the class. For example, in dealing with daily temperatures, if the true class limits are 79.5° and 89.5°, then 84.5° should be used to represent the class in computing the mean. When possible, it is best to compute the mean and other statistics directly from the raw data rather than use the grouped formulas, though sometimes there is no choice, as when calculating statistics based on published data tables in which variables have already been grouped.

A closely related measure is a *weighted mean.* In most data collection situations, each element is sampled with equal probability. However, sometimes there is intentional oversampling of parts of a population. For example, say the goal of a study is to compare death rates from a particular illness in southern and northern hospitals, and say that 20% of the hospitals in the United States are in the south versus 80% in the north. If resources permitted studying a total of 100 hospitals, equal-probability sampling would lead to selecting about 20 hospitals in the south. That would be too small a sample for reliable inferences about death rates in southern hospitals. In this situation, the researcher might choose to double-sample southern hospitals, so 40 are selected rather than 20. Choosing 40 hospitals in the south and 60 in the north would ensure enough coverage of both areas to permit calculating statistics for each region. Separate means for southern and northern hospitals would be computed using the usual mean formula. However, southern hospitals are being oversampled, so a special "weighted" formula is needed for computing the national mean.

The formula for the weighted mean is

$$\overline{X} = \sum (X_i w_i) / \sum w_i,$$

where $w_i$ represents the weight of the $i$th observation. The weights compensate for the higher chances for selecting some observations than others. The weight for the $i$th observation would be

$$w_i = p_i N / f_i,$$

where $f_i$ is the frequency of category $i$ in the sample and $p_i$ is the known population proportion in that category. If a sample includes 40 hospitals in the south, then southern hospitals were double-sampled (40 rather than 20), and so each hospital should be weighted by the factor of .50 (= .20 × 100/40). Northern hospitals were correspondingly undersampled (60 instead of 80), so they should be weighted by a factor of 1.33 (= .80 × 100/60).

Many public opinion surveys purposely oversample particular parts of the population and then use a "weight variable" to compensate. For example, the 1964 American National Election Study double-sampled blacks in order to have more interviews to describe attitudes of African-Americans. The data file for that study includes the weights (the $w_i$) needed for computing overall means and other statistics.

Another common weighting situation occurs when there are several samples with separate means for each, but a *pooled* mean is of interest. The samples may not be of equal size, so calculating the overall mean requires weighting each separate mean by the number of cases on which it is based. For example, say a variable is measured for each of 3 years, with 1,000 people being in the sample for the first year, 800 for the next year, and 500 for the third year. Because the number of cases for each year is different, it would be inappropriate to add up

TABLE 3.4
Pooled Mean Calculation

| Year | Sample Size (N) | Mean ($\overline{X}$) | Sum of $X = N\overline{X}$ | Variance |
|------|-----------------|-----------------------|----------------------------|----------|
| 2001 | 1,000 | 1.3 | 1,300.00 | .25 |
| 2002 | 800 | 1.1 | 880.00 | .36 |
| 2003 | 500 | 0.9 | 450.00 | .16 |
| Total | 2,300 | | 2,630 | |

Mean of means = (1.3 + 1.1 + 0.9)/3     = 1.100
Pooled mean = [(1.3 × 1,000) + (1.1 × 800) + (0.9 × 500)]/ 2,300 = 2,630/ 2,300   = 1.143
Pooled variance = [(999 × 0.25) + (799 × 0.36) + (499 × 0.16)]/2,297   = 0.269

the separate yearly means and divide by the number of years. Instead, a combined mean should reflect the unequal numbers of cases underlying each mean, giving greater weight to the years with more people studied. For a pooled mean, use the following formula:

$$\overline{X} = \sum (N_j \overline{X}_j)/\sum N_j,$$

where $\overline{X}_j$ is the mean for sample $j$, and $N_j$ is the number of cases in sample $j$. An example of the calculation of a pooled mean is given in Table 3.4.

*The Mean for Dichotomous Data.* Should dichotomous data be summarized by modes, medians, or means? The answer is that each can be used. The mode shows which of the two categories occurs more often, as does the rough median. The mean has a more special interpretation.

Score the dichotomous variable as 1 for one category (called a *success*) and 0 for the other category. The mean then shows the proportion of cases that fall in the "1" category. If the proportion of cases with the score of 1 is denoted as $p$, then the mean of the dichotomous variable is

$$\overline{X} = p.$$

To see this, use the mean formula for grouped data. The number of observations with a score of 1 would be $pN$, and the remaining $N - pN$ observations would have a score of 0. The mean is then

TABLE 3.5
Church Attendance Distribution

| Attendance | Code | Frequency | Proportion |
|---|---|---|---|
| Attended | 1 | 30 | $.15 = p$ |
| Did not attend | 0 | 170 | $.85 = 1 - p$ |
| Total | | 200 | 1.00 |
| Mean | $.15 = [(30 \times 1) + (170 \times 0)]/200$ | | $= p$ |
| Variance | $.1275 = .15 \times .85$ | | $= p(1 - p)$ |
| Standard deviation | $.3571$ | | |

$$\bar{X} = \{[1 \times (pN)] + [0 \times (N - pN)]\}/N = [(pN) + 0]/N = pN/N = p.$$

Take, for example, church attendance—whether or not a person went to church during the past week. Say that only 15% of the public went to church (see Table 3.5). The modal category is "not going to church." Likewise, the median person did not go to church. If the variable is scored as 1 for "attended" and 0 for "did not attend," the mean would be .15, showing that 15% of the people attended. The 1/0 scoring of the dichotomous variable (known as creating a *dummy variable*) leads to a mean with an intuitive interpretation—the proportion of cases that fall in the category scored 1.

## Discussion

*Comparisons of Mean, Median, and Mode.* Table 3.6 summarizes several of the properties of the mode, median, and mean that have been discussed in this chapter. The chart also rates these measures according to the various criteria for summary statistics that were presented in Chapter 1. Some of the conclusions in Table 3.6 are debatable, but it still gives a useful beginning point. Further technical properties of these measures will be presented at the end of Chapter 5.

The choice among the three classic measures of center depends mainly on two considerations: the distribution of the values on the variable, and the level of measurement.

First, there are different possible shapes of distributions for metric variables. One of these is the symmetric unimodal distribution as in

TABLE 3.6
Properties of Measures of Center

| | *Mode* | *Median* | *Mean* |
|---|---|---|---|
| Level of measurement | nominal or higher | ordinal or higher | metric (usually) |
| Rigidly defined | yes | yes | yes |
| Based on all cases | minimally | yes | best |
| Simple to understand | yes | yes | yes |
| Easy to calculate | best | yes | yes |
| Algebraic | no | no | yes |
| Stable under sampling | no | yes | best |
| Single valued | not always | yes | best |
| Resistant to outliers | yes | yes | no |
| Generalize to two-variable statistics | no | no | yes |
| Insensitive to combining categories | no | yes | yes |
| Computed for open-ended variables | indeterminate | yes | indeterminate |
| Equal to actual data values | yes | for odd $N$ | not always |
| Interpretation: | most typical value | middle value | average value |
| Bad guess interpretation: | highest % accuracy | closest to all scores | minimize sum of signed deviations |

Figure 3.1, section a. In this instance, the mode, the median, and the mean are all at the center of the distribution. Because the mode, median, and mean are all equal for a symmetric unimodal distribution, the choice among them would not matter.

A contrasting case is a *skewed* distribution, as in section b. Here small values predominate, but there are some atypical large values. This is called *positive skew* because the tail of the distribution goes off to the right. The mode is the value that occurs most frequently. The middle case is higher, so the median is larger. Also, the average is affected by the outliers, so the mean is larger yet. Thus, the mode is smallest, the median second, and the mean largest for positive skewed distributions. By contrast, a distribution with a *negative skew* (section c) has mostly large values, with some atypical small values; the mode is largest, the median second, and the mean smallest. The median is often used to summarize skewed numeric data because the mean can be strongly affected by outliers.[5]

36

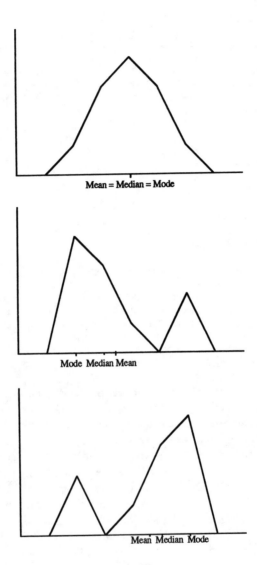

Figure 3.1. Section A. Symmetric Distribution
Section B. Positively Skewed Distribution
Section C. Negatively Skewed Distribution

There was a strong positive skew in our example involving the numbers of wars in which different nations fought (Table 3.1) because of the outlier nation that had been in 50 wars. The values of the measures of center follow the pattern for positively skewed variables: the mode is 1, the median is 3, and the mean is 10. The median value is more typical of the distribution as a whole that the mean is. The median is generally much nearer the mean than to the mode (Yule & Kendall, 1968: 117), although this example shows that that rule does not always hold.

Besides the shape of the distribution of values, the level of measurement must be considered in choosing which of these measures of center to use. The simplest rule is to use the mode for nominal data, the median for ordinal data, and the mean for metric data. Additionally, a lower-level statistic can be safely used for higher-level data, as in using the mode for ordinal data and the median for metric data.

There is actually considerable controversy over using numeric-based statistics, like means, on ordinal data. The strict level of measurement rule is that means should never be computed on ordinal data, but such analysis has become common. Those researchers willing to take the mean of an ordinal variable argue that there are latent continuous variables (albeit with error at the manifest level) underlying ordinal variables (Borgatta & Bohrnstedt, 1980), and that integer scoring of ordinal variables (assigning the score of 1 to the first category, 2 to the second, and so on) usually yields statistical results that would be fairly close to what would be obtained for the true unknown numbered categories (Labovitz, 1970). By contrast, statistical purists argue that there is a chance of making a serious statistical fallacy, because results based on integer scoring could be very different from those based on the true underlying scoring (Grether, 1976). This controversy is unlikely to be resolved anytime soon (Mayer, 1971). In the meantime, it is best to stick close to the level of measurement of the data as a first step and acknowledge directly when violating that level.

In looking at variables, do not feel that it is always necessary to select a single measure of center. The different measures provide different pieces of information, and sometimes it is useful to look at these multiple aspects of the data. Thus, in the war example used throughout this chapter, the median might be the best choice if just one measure were to be reported, but the mode and mean also give relevant information. Multiple measures are shown below the tables in this monograph so readers can compare the results provided by each.

There are some additional measures of center, but they are used less frequently, so some readers might want to skip forward to the next chapter.

*Mathematical Properties of Measures of Center.* The mean, median, and mode on metric data can be transformed by a linear rule: Adding a constant $k$ to every value on the variable increases the center by that amount $k$, and multiplying every value by a constant $m$ multiplies the center by $m$. Mathematically,

$$\text{Center } (k + mX_i) = k + [m \times \text{Center}(X_i)].$$

As an example, if a variable $X$ is measured on a scale of 0 to 100, with 50 as neutral point, and if the researcher wanted to convert the variable to a scale of $-100$ to $+100$, with 0 as neutral point, the conversion rule would be $2X - 100$, with the mean score being translated as $2\overline{X} - 100$.

## Other Order-Based Measures of Center

The interest in exploratory data analysis has led to the development of several new order-based measures of center. In line with the philosophy behind exploratory data analysis, these measures are useful in providing an understanding of the center of the variable. They tend to be particularly resistant to the influence of extreme values. That is, their values are not thrown far off because of outliers.

Some of these measures require prior calculation of the quartile values. Recall that the bottom quartile ($Q_1$) is where the 25th percentile hits, and the top quartile ($Q_3$) is where the 75th percentile hits. There are actually two different ways of locating quartiles. One (Tukey, 1977) is that the bottom quartile corresponds to the $(N + 1)/4$th case and the top to the $3(N + 1)/4$th case. These are easy formulas to use, but they often yield quartiles that are between data values. For example, with six cases, the first quartile would be the 1¾th case, three quarters of the way up from the bottom case toward the second case. The other way of locating the quartiles (Velleman & Hoaglin, 1981) is to say that they are the medians of the cases up to and including the median. For six cases, the median is between the third and fourth cases, so according to this definition the first quartile is the middle of the first three cases (i.e., case 2) and the third quartile is the middle of the highest three cases (i.e., case 5). The first definitional system is used in the examples in this book.

One set of EDA-based measures involves averages of percentile values. The *midextreme* or *midrange* is the average of the smallest and largest values:

$$\text{Midextreme} = (X_{minimum} + X_{maximum})/2.$$

Returning to the war example in Table 3.1, section a, the largest value is 50 and the smallest is 1, so the midextreme is 25.5 wars. The *midhinge* is the average of the bottom and top quartiles:

$$\text{Midhinge} = (Q_1 + Q_3)/2.$$

In this example, the bottom quartile value is 1 and the top quartile value is 9, so the midhinge is their average, 5 wars. More generally, the average of the scores of the bottom $x$th percentile and the top $x$th percentile gives a *midsummary*. The midextreme, midhinge, and other midsummaries can be used as measures of center.

Comparing these different midsummary statistics (Velleman and Hoaglin, 1981) gives an indication of the degree of symmetry of the distribution. In a symmetric distribution, the midextreme, midhinge, median, and all the other midsummaries would be equal. If the variable is skewed with some unusually high cases, the midextreme would be higher than the midhinge, which would be higher than the median (as in the war example). If the variable is skewed with some unusually low cases, this ordering would be reversed.

Another EDA-based measure of center is known as the *trimean* (Tukey, 1977: 46) or *best easy systematic (BES) estimate*. It is a combination of the median and the quartile values, weighting the median more heavily than the quartiles. The formula or the trimean is:

$$\text{Trimean} = [Q_1 + (2X_{median}) + Q_3]/4.$$

In the war example, the first quartile is 1, the median is 3, and the top quartile is 9, so the trimean equals 4. The trimean is actually the average of the median and the midhinge defined above. An advantage of the trimean as a measure of center is that it combines the median's emphasis on center values with the midhinge's attention to the extremes.

Some computer programs produce one further EDA-based central-tendency statistic, the *biweight* or *bisquare weight*. Its formula (Velleman, 1989: 77) is too complicated to calculate by hand. Mosteller and Tukey (1977: 206-207, 352-356) report the biweight has a low variance from sample to sample, is resistant to the effects of extreme values (as is the median), and is responsive to changes in the middle of its range (as is the mean). It may be useful for exploring data distributions, but it is very nonintuitive.

## Other Means

The regular mean discussed above (known technically as the *arithmetic mean*) is the most commonly used average, but there are some other "averages" that are used to avoid the effects of outliers or to handle particular types of ratio-level data.

*Trimmed Means.* Two ways around the sensitivity of the mean to extreme cases are to *trim* or *winsorize* the outliers from the data before computing the mean. Trimming the data involves removing the most extreme values entirely, as is done in Olympic diving competitions when the top and bottom scores given by the panel of judges to a dive are tossed out before the mean evaluation of the dive is computed. Winsorizing the data instead involves changing the most extreme values to equal the next less extreme values. As examples, the *5% trimmed mean* drops the highest 5% and lowest 5% of the observations before computing the mean, whereas the *5% winsorized mean* with 20 observations changes the highest value (the highest 5%) to the second highest value and changes the lowest value (the lowest 5%) to the second lowest. These are ad hoc solutions, but they are often effective in improving the resistance of the mean.[6] To express these statistics mathematically requires first sorting the variable so that its values are in order from smallest $(X_1)$ to largest $(X_N)$. Then the $j/N$th trimmed mean, $T(j)$, is

$$T(j/N) = \frac{1}{N - 2j} \sum_{i=j+1}^{N-j} X_i,$$

and the $j/N$th winsorized mean, $W(j)$, is

$$W(j/N) = \frac{1}{N}(jX_{j+1} + \sum_{i=j+1}^{N-j} X_i + jX_{N-j}).$$

One trimmed mean has been proposed as an alternative statistic to the mean. The *midmean* is the average of the central half of the observations. If the observations have been sorted into numerical order, then the formula for the midmean is

$$\text{Midmean} = \frac{2}{N} \sum_{i=N/4}^{3N/4} X_i.$$

This statistic is much more resistant to extreme values than is the mean, though some statisticians would feel that it ignores the extreme cases too much. Rosenberger and Gasko (1983) examined the properties of several trimmed measures, finding the midmean has the most desirable properties.

*Geometric Mean.* Special means are sometimes used for ratio data. The *geometric mean* is used to summarize a variable when relative change is being measured. Whereas the arithmetic mean adds the different values on the variable before dividing by the number of cases, the geometric mean multiplies together the different values and then takes the root corresponding to the number of cases. The formula for the geometric mean (GM) is

$$\text{GM} = \left( \prod_{i=1}^{N} X_i \right)^{\frac{1}{N}}$$

where the capital pi stands for multiplying the $X_i$ values together. For example, consider the numbers 2 and 8. Their arithmetic average is 5. Their geometric mean is 4, obtained by multiplying the two numbers together (2 times 8 is 16) and then taking the second root of that product (the square root of 16 is 4). If three numbers were being multiplied together, the cube root of their product would be taken, and so on.

The geometric mean is useful when the values of a variable increase exponentially over time. That is often the case for the growth of amounts of money. Say the budget for a public agency doubled one year and increased eightfold the next year (see Table 3.7). Over the two years, its budget would have increased by a factor of 16, as

TABLE 3.7
Means for Growth Rates

| | Section A. Agency Budget Growth | |
| Year | Budget | Growth Rate |
|---|---|---|
| 2000 | $100,000 | |
| 2001 | $200,000 | 2 |
| 2002 | $1,600,000 | 8 |
| Arithmetic mean | | 5 = (2 + 8)/2 |
| Geometric mean | | 4 = sqrt (2 × 8) |

| | Section B. Effects of 5% Annual Growth Rate | |
| Year | Budget | Growth Rate |
|---|---|---|
| 2000 | $100,000 | |
| 2001 | $500,000 | 5 |
| 2002 | $2,500,000 | 5 |

| | Section C. Effects of 4% Annual Growth Rate | |
| Year | Budget | Growth Rate |
|---|---|---|
| 2000 | $100,000 | |
| 2001 | $400,000 | 4 |
| 2002 | $1,600,000 | 4 |

shown in section a. But what is the average annual growth rate for that agency? The arithmetic average would obtain the wrong answer. The arithmetic mean of 2 and 8 is 5, but if the agency's budget had increased by a multiple of 5 two years in a row, its budget would have increased by a factor of 25 (section b), not the observed factor of 16. The geometric mean of 2 and 8 is 4, and indeed the agency experienced the same growth as if its budget had quadrupled both years (section c). The geometric mean properly captures the average growth rate over the two years, whereas the arithmetic mean does not measure any aspect of the budget process.

An alternate way of computing the geometric mean involves using logarithms. Recall that the logarithm of a product is the sum of the logarithms, and that the log of the $N$th root of $X$ is $(1/N)\log X$. Therefore, the geometric mean can be obtained by taking the logarithms of all the values, computing the arithmetic average of the logarithms, and then taking the antilogarithm of the result. That is,

$$\log(GM) = \text{Average } [\log(X_i)],$$

so

$$GM = \exp\{\text{Average } [\log(X_i)]\},$$

where "average" is meant as the arithmetic average.

The logarithmic version of the equation implies that the geometric mean weights values extra the closer they are to 1. Values much greater than 1 (and very small fractions) have less effect on the geometric mean than values near 1, which is why the geometric mean of 4 is closer to the value of 2 than to 8 in the example above.[7]

*Harmonic Mean.* Another average for numeric data is the *harmonic mean*, which is used when averaging rates. Whereas the arithmetic mean takes the average of the values of a variable, the harmonic mean (HM) is based on the reciprocals of the values. It is the reciprocal of the mean of reciprocals:

$$HM = \frac{1}{\frac{1}{N}\sum_{i=1}^{N}\frac{1}{X_i}} = \frac{N}{\sum \frac{1}{X_i}}.$$

The harmonic mean is used mainly to average different rates. Say that in the year 2000 it takes 3 months for Chicago to reach 150 murders, a rate of 50 murders per month. Say that same year it takes Detroit 5 months to reach 150 murders, a rate of 30 murders a month. What is the average murder rate for the two cities combined? It might appear that 40 murders per month is the answer, but that is not the case. All in all, the two cities experienced 300 murders in 8 months, which is an average rate of 37.5 murders per month (see Table 3.8). How can this be the case? Detroit took longer getting to 150 murders at a slower rate, and the longer time at the slower rate pulls down the average rate. To compute this as a harmonic mean, use

$$1/\{[(1/\text{rate}_1) + (1/\text{rate}_2)]/2\} = 1/\{[(1/30) + (1/50)]/2\}$$
$$= 1/\{[(8/150)]/2\} = 1/(4/150) = 150/4 = 37.5.$$

The formula for the harmonic mean also can be represented as taking the reciprocals of each value, computing the arithmetic average of those reciprocals, and then taking the reciprocal of the result. That is,

44

## TABLE 3.8
### Murder Rates in Two Cities

| City | Murders | Time (# of months) | Rate (per month) |
|------|---------|--------------------|------------------|
| Chicago | 150 | 3 | 50 |
| Detroit | 150 | 5 | 30 |
| Total | 300 | 8 | |
| Arithmetic mean | | 40 = (50 + 30)/2 | |
| Harmonic mean | | 37.5 = 2/[(1/50) + (1/30)] | |

$$\text{reciprocal (HM)} = \text{Average [reciprocal } (X_i)],$$

so

$$\text{HM} = \text{reciprocal \{Average [reciprocal } (X_i)]\}}.$$

The harmonic mean gives greatest weight to smaller values, be-cause the reciprocal of a smaller number is larger than the reciprocal of a larger number. This effect is evident in the above examples, where the harmonic mean is closer to the smaller rates (30) than to the larger rates (50).

A basic result is that the geometric mean is always between the val-ues of the harmonic and arithmetic means: $\text{HM} \leq \text{GM} \leq \overline{X}$.

*Generalized Mean.* The alternative formulas given above for the geometric and harmonic mean suggest a more general formulation of a mean. Let T represent a transformation (such as taking a logarithm, or a reciprocal, or a square) and let $M$ denote a *generalized mean.* Then,

$$T(M) = \text{Average [T}(X_i)].$$

Define $T^{-1}$ as the inverse of transformation T—the transformation that undoes the original transformation—so that $T^{-1}[T(X)] = X$. As an example, a square root is the inverse of a square operation. The gen-eralized mean $M$ can then be expressed as

$$M = T^{-1} \{\text{Average [T}(X_i)]\}.$$

The geometric mean is one special case of this formulation, where T is the logarithmic transformation and the inverse $T^{-1}$ of the logarithm is the antilog (also called exponentiation) transformation. The harmonic mean is another special case, where T is the reciprocal and the inverse $T^{-1}$ of the reciprocal is again a reciprocal transformation—because $1/(1/X) = X$. The arithmetic mean also fits this formulation, where T is the identity transformation [$T(X) = X$] and $T^{-1}$ is also the identity transformation.

The generalized mean formulation suggests that the algebraic, geometric, and harmonic means are just three of a larger set of possible means. As a final example of this general formulation, consider the *quadratic mean* (QM), also known as the *root mean square*. Let the transformation T be squaring a value, so the inverse $T^{-1}$ of that transformation is the square-root transformation. Then,

$$\text{square (QM)} = \text{Average [square}(X_i)],$$

so

$$QM = \sqrt{\text{Average [square}(X_i)]} = \sqrt{\text{Average } [(X_i)^2]} \, .$$

The quadratic mean gives more weight to values with greater magnitudes—large positive and large negative numbers. It will be employed in the discussion of measures of spread for metric variables in Chapter 4.

The geometric mean, harmonic mean, and quadratic mean cannot be transformed by a linear transformation in the way that the mean, median, and mode can. Actually, these three generalized means are transformed appropriately by a multiplier [$\text{Center}(mX_i) = m \times \text{Center}(X_i)$] but not by a constant added to each value [$\text{Center}(k + X_i) \neq k + \text{Center}(X_i)$]. This shows that these means are appropriate only for ratio-level data and not interval data.

*Summary.* Several different measures of center can be used on numeric data. The most common is the mean, with the median being used when there is an outlier and when the variable is unbounded at an extreme. Special averages are appropriate for dealing with relative growth and with rates. EDA-based measures also are useful for dealing with outliers.

# 4. MEASURES OF SPREAD

Central tendency is just one property of interest in summarizing the distribution of a variable. Not only do we want to find the typical value for a variable, but we want to know how typical that value is. This concern moves us along to consider the spread of the variable.

The most important measures of spread have been developed for numeric data—the closely related *variance* and *standard deviation* statistics. Other measures have been developed for dealing with dispersion at the lower levels of measurement by adapting the concept of variation.

Measures of spread increase in value with greater variation on the variable. They all equal zero when there is no dispersion. Maximum variation for metric and ordinal variables is defined as occurring when the cases are evenly split between two extreme categories—*polarization*. Maximum dispersion for nominal variables is defined either as when there is an even distribution of cases across the categories regardless of the number of categories (*uniformity*) or when each category occurs just once (*individuality*). Examples of these definitions will be given in this chapter.

Another complexity in dealing with spread measures is their abstract quality. It is not intuitively clear, for example, what meaning to give to a spread of 10. As a result, it is common to norm spread values. One norming procedure is to divide the obtained spread value by the maximum possible spread for the statistic, so a value of 1 represents maximal spread. Another norming procedure, used in the coefficient of variation and other statistics, is to divide the spread by the corresponding central-tendency value; this sometimes is described as yielding an *absolute* measure of dispersion (Yule & Kendall, 1968: 143) because the variable's unit of measurement is removed. Norming procedures will be used several times below.

## Standard Deviation
## and Other Deviation-Based Measures of Spread

The major measures of spread for metric data are based on deviations from the mean value. Metric data have a unit of measurement, so a deviation shows by how many units the observation differs from the mean:

$$d_i = X_i - \overline{X}.$$

For example, if the mean number of prior convictions of a set of criminal defendants is 4, then the deviation for a defendant with 20 previous convictions is 16 (= 20 − 4), and the deviation for a defendant without any prior convictions is −4 (= 0 − 4). Several spread measures have been devised to summarize the size of these deviations by averaging them—averaging either the raw deviations, absolute deviations, or squared deviations. Each of these possibilities will be described below. The major measures of spread for metric data are the closely related variance and standard deviation statistics,[8] but it is useful to discuss the mean deviation first.

*Mean Deviation and Variants.* A simple measure of dispersion would seem to be the average deviation from the mean:

$$\sum (X_i - \overline{X})/N = \sum d_i/N.$$

Recall, however, from the discussion of the properties of the mean in Chapter 3 that the sum of the deviations around the mean is always zero. As a result, the average of the deviations from the mean would equal zero for any variable. For example, Table 4.1 shows the numbers of prior convictions of 10 prisoners. If eight defendants had 0 prior convictions and two had 20, the average number of prior convictions is 4. The sum of deviations is 8 × (−4) + 2 × (16) = −32 + 32 = 0, so the average deviation around the mean is zero (see Table 4.1, column 3). Because it is always zero by definition, the average deviation around the mean cannot indicate which distribution of values has greater spread.

Deviations from the mean would yield a more useful measure of dispersion if instead we averaged the absolute values of the deviations from the mean. This is called the *mean deviation* or *average deviation*. The formula is

$$\text{MD} = \sum |X_i - \overline{X}|/N = \sum |d_i|/N.$$

The mean deviation has a minimum of $R/N$ and a maximum of $R/2$, where $R$ is the range of the data (the largest value minus the smallest one).

In the criminal example (see Table 4.1), if eight defendants had no previous convictions and the other two had 20 each, the sum of absolute deviations would be 64 (4 for each of eight defendants, plus 16 each for two more defendants), and the mean deviation would then be

TABLE 4.1
Deviation-Based Measures of Spread

| Defendant | # of Prior Convictions | Deviation | Absolute Deviation | Squared Deviation | Squared Value |
|-----------|------------------------|-----------|--------------------|--------------------|----------------|
| Defendant A | 0 | −4 | 4 | 16 | 0 |
| Defendant B | 0 | −4 | 4 | 16 | 0 |
| Defendant C | 0 | −4 | 4 | 16 | 0 |
| Defendant D | 0 | −4 | 4 | 16 | 0 |
| Defendant E | 0 | −4 | 4 | 16 | 0 |
| Defendant F | 0 | −4 | 4 | 16 | 0 |
| Defendant G | 0 | −4 | 4 | 16 | 0 |
| Defendant H | 0 | −4 | 4 | 16 | 0 |
| Defendant I | 20 | 16 | 16 | 256 | 400 |
| Defendant J | 20 | 16 | 16 | 256 | 400 |
| | | | | | |
| Sum | 40 | 0 | 64 | 640 | 800 |
| Mean | 4 | 0 | 6.4 | 64 = variance | |
| | | | | 8 = standard deviation | |

Mean = 40/10-4
Variance = $[800-(40^2/10)]/10-[800-160]/10-640/10-64$
Standard deviation = $\sqrt{(64)} = 8$
Coefficient of variation = 8/4 = 2
Gini's mean difference = 320/45 = 7.11

Median = 0
Mean deviation = 64/10 = 6.4
Average absolute deviation from the median = 40/10 = 4
MAD = 0

6.4. That value captures the notion of measuring the typical dispersion well.

The mean deviation is a plausible measure of dispersion. It shows how far off the data values are, on average, from the mean value, when signs of deviations are ignored. However, the mean deviation is not used often. For one thing, dealing with absolute values turns out not to lead to useful generalizations when we move into statistics for more than one variable. For another, the mean deviation around the mean does not have any special statistical uniqueness properties; recall from Chapter 3 that the average absolute deviation is actually minimal when the deviations are taken from the median rather than from the mean. The mean deviation would be an intuitively appealing statistic, but it lacks attractive mathematical properties.

*The Variance and Standard Deviation of a Population.* A better way of working with deviations from the mean is to square them. Whereas taking absolute values leads to awkward algebraic manipulations when we generalize past one variable, squaring leads to useful statistical properties. As a result, the usual way of measuring spread for metric variables involves squaring the deviations from the mean and averaging these squared deviations. This is termed the *variance* of the variable. (Actually, this definition is for the variance parameter for the full population; estimating the variance statistic on the basis of a smaller sample from that population requires slight modification of this formulation as will be shown in the next section.)

The population variance is the average squared deviation from the mean:

$$\sigma^2 = \sum (X_i - \mu)^2 / N = \sum d_i^2 / N,$$

where the Greek letter $\sigma^2$ (sigma squared) is used to represent the population variance and the Greek letter $\mu$ (mu) is used to represent the population mean.

The variance statistic is unusual in an important sense—the squaring operation means that the variance is not in the original units of measurement. For example, if we were measuring the gross domestic products of countries in dollars, the variance would be in squared dollars. We can return to the original unit of measurement by taking the square root of the variance. The resulting statistic, termed the *standard deviation*, is a very common measure of spread. The formula for the population standard deviation is

$$\sigma = \sqrt{\sum (X_i - \mu)^2 / N} = \sqrt{\sum d_i^2 / N}.$$

As an example, consider again the previous convictions of criminal defendants as shown in Table 4.1. The mean number of convictions is 4. The first eight defendants had 4 convictions less than the mean, leading to squared deviations of 16. The last two defendants had 16 convictions more than the mean, leading to squared deviations of 256. The squared deviations sum to $(8 \times 16) + (2 \times 256) = 128 + 512 = 640$. The average squared deviation is then $640/10 = 64$, which is the variance (see Table 4.1). Because that variance is in the unusual unit of "squared convictions," we would take its square root to obtain a standard deviation of 8 convictions.

Although the above formulas for variance and standard deviation in terms of deviations from the mean are easy to follow conceptually, they are difficult to employ when doing hand calculations. For example, it would be painful to calculate squared deviations from a mean of 2.634. Fortunately, there are computational formulas for the variance and standard deviation that are easier to employ. Three equivalent computational formulas for the population variance are

$$\sigma^2 = [\sum (X_i^2) - (1/N) (\sum X)^2]/N$$

$$= [\sum (X_i^2) - N(\overline{X})^2]/N$$

$$= \sum (X_i^2)/N - \overline{X}^2,$$

and the computational formulas for the standard deviation are the square roots of those formulas.

The computational formulas involve summing squared data values, which is not the same as squaring the sum of the data values. For example, say the data values are 1 and 2; their sum is 3, so the squared sum of the data values is 9. However, the squares of the data values are 1 and 4, which adds to 5, and that is the sum of squared data values used before the minus sign in the computational formulas. Scientific calculators can compute sums of $X$ and $X^2$ with fewer operations than required if deviations from the mean were used.

The computational version can easily be shown to be equivalent to the definitional formula. First, expand the squared deviation:

$$(X_i - \overline{X})^2 = X_i^2 - 2\overline{X}X_i + \overline{X}^2.$$

The variance then can be represented as

$$\sigma^2 = \sum (X_i - \overline{X})^2/N = \sum (X_i^2 - 2\overline{X}X_i + \overline{X}^2)/N$$

$$= \sum X_i^2/N - 2\sum \overline{X}X_i/N + \sum \overline{X}^2/N.$$

Since $\overline{X}$ is a constant, it can be moved before the summation sign, so

$$\sigma^2 = \sum X_i^2/N - 2\overline{X} \sum X_i/N + N\overline{X}^2/N.$$

Notice that the formula for the mean appears in the middle term, permitting simplification of that term; also the last term can be simplified. This gives

TABLE 4.2
Housing Price Data for Three Cities (in dollars)

| | City A | City B | City C |
|---|---|---|---|
| | 96,000 | 45,000 | 45,000 |
| | 101,000 | 83,000 | 47,000 |
| | 105,000 | 100,000 | 43,000 |
| | 99,000 | 117,000 | 155,000 |
| | 101,000 | 150,000 | 154,000 |
| | 98,000 | 105,000 | 156,000 |
| Mean | 100,000 | 100,000 | 100,000 |
| Variance | 8,000,000 | 1,021,333,333 | 3,026,666,667 |
| Standard deviation | 2,828.43 | 31,958.31 | 55,015.15 |
| Coefficient of variation | .03 | .32 | .55 |

$$\sigma^2 = \sum X_i^2/N - 2\overline{X}^2 + \overline{X}^2 = \sum X_i^2/N - \overline{X}^2.$$

Returning to the criminal defendants example with eight defendants having no convictions and two having 20 convictions, the variance calculation would entail summing the square of 0 eight times (which leads to a partial sum of 0) and summing the square of 20 twice (2 × 400 = 800) to get a sum of squares of 800. Next, sum the actual values (40), square that sum ($40^2$ = 1,600), and divide that by the number of cases (10) to get 160. To calculate the variance, subtract the latter (160) from the sum of squares (800) to obtain 640, and divide by the number of cases (10) to get 64. The standard deviation is, of course, still the square root of the variance, or 8 convictions.

The standard deviation is increased by outliers. Thus, in the above example, the standard deviation of 8 is larger than the mean deviation of 6.4, because squaring deviations increases the impact of the large deviations caused by outliers. This lack of resistance to outliers could be seen as a problem with the standard-deviation measure, but the advantage of working with squares rather than absolute values more than compensates, so the standard deviation is the usual measure of spread.

As another example, Table 4.2 shows hypothetical prices for houses sold in three cities during the past week, along with the means and variances for each city. These cities have the same mean housing price, but the variances differ. The house prices in city A show very little dispersion; there is greater dispersion in city B; city C seems sharply split between expensive housing and inexpensive housing. This example also shows why it is useful to summarize a distribution in terms of its spread as well as its center: These three cities have identical centers, but their different spreads call attention to differences in the distributions of prices in these cities.

Several further interpretations can be given to the variance and standard deviation. First, the standard deviation is often interpreted as a *root mean square deviation*. Recall the discussion of the quadratic mean in the previous chapter—it is the square root of the average squared values. The standard deviation is similar, except that it squares the deviations from the mean rather than raw data values. The standard deviation is the square root of the average squared deviations, so it is a quadratic mean of the deviations, also known as the root mean square deviation.

A second interpretation of the variance and standard deviation is based on what is termed a *least-squares* logic (Blalock, 1972: 59). One property of the mean mentioned in Chapter 3 was that the sum of squared deviations around it is minimal. We can restate that as a property of the variance: *The variance calculated around the mean is smaller than the average squared deviation around any other value.* This minimization is a special property of the variance. Recall that the average deviation around the mean is not minimal; the only dispersion statistics calculated off the mean that are minimal are the variance and standard deviation.

A third interpretation of the variance and standard deviation involves another possible measure of spread—the average squared difference between all pairs of observations:

$$\sum (X_i - X_j)^2 / \binom{N}{2}$$

where the binomial coefficient in the denominator reduces to $N(N - 1)/2$. It can be shown (Hays, 1963: 180) that this average squared difference equals $2\sigma^2 N/(N - 1)$; therefore, *the variance is proportional to the average squared difference between all pairs of observations.* The more that pairs of cases are unequal in their scores, the higher the variance and standard deviation of the set of scores. Indeed, if we took the average squared difference between all pairs of observations, including the observation with itself (Yule & Kendall, 1968: 147), we would have $\Sigma(X_i - X_j)^2 / N^2 = 2\sigma^2$. Thus the standard deviation is proportional to the root mean square of all the possible pairs of differences:

$$\sigma = (1/\sqrt{2N}) \times \sqrt{\sum (X_i - X_j)^2/N}.$$

That leads to the question of when the variance and standard deviation are maximal. According to the result just obtained, they are maximal when the average squared difference between all pairs of observations is maximal. That turns out to be when the data are polarized, with half the observations at the maximum and the other half at the minimum, because the squared deviations from the mean are then maximal. Say there are an even number ($N$) of observations, exactly $N/2$ of these observations equal $X_{max}$ and the other $N/2$ observations equal $X_{min}$. The deviations $(X_{max} - \overline{X}) = d = (\overline{X} - X_{min})$, so the sum of squared deviations from the mean is $Nd^2$. The population variance is $d^2$ and the standard deviation would be $d$. For example, a variable that could range from 0 to 100 would have its maximum variance if its mean were 50, half the cases were 0, and the other half 100. Its variance would be 2,500 and its standard deviation would be 50. More generally, if we let $R$ represent the range of the variable ($R = X_{max} - X_{min}$), then the maximum variance is $(R/2)^2$ and the maximum standard deviation is $R/2$.

A further property of the variance should be mentioned here: Variances are additive under one special circumstance. *If two variables are strictly independent of one another, then the variance of their sum equals the sum of their variances.* If, for example, one variance is labeled A and the other is labeled B, then the variance of their sum is

$$\sigma_{A+B}^2 = \sigma_A^2 + \sigma_B^2$$

if A and B are independent of one another. This rule is important because it sometimes permits the decomposition of the variance of a variable $X$ into separate parts that are due to independent elements, as will be discussed below. Note, incidentally, that this rule for variances does not apply for standard deviations:

$$\sigma_{A+B} = \sqrt{\sigma_A^2 + \sigma_B^2} \neq \sigma_A + \sigma_B.$$

The standard deviation satisfies most of Yule and Kendall's rules for good statistics listed in Chapter 1—it is rigidly defined, based on all the observations, algebraic, and minimally affected by sampling fluctuation. However, it is awkward to compute, not resistant to extreme values, and, more important, it is not readily comprehended. The mean deviation is fairly simple to understand, but the standard deviation is so abstract that its values are more difficult to interpret. Yet the standard deviation is the most important measure of spread for metric variables. The usefulness of the standard deviation will become more clear shortly.

*The Variance and Standard Deviation of a Sample.* Technically, the variance and standard deviation have been defined so far for full populations, rather than for samples of cases. However, the variance and standard deviation thus defined lack some optimal properties when dealing with samples. This problem will be discussed in Chapter 5 more directly, but here it suffices to say that a simple modification of the definitional formula is required for samples. Instead of dividing the sum of squared deviations by the number of cases, the sum of squared deviations should be divided by the number of cases less 1. The formulas for the sample versions of the variance (denoted as $s^2$) and standard deviation (denoted as $s$) are

$$s^2 = \sum (X_i - \overline{X})^2/(N - 1) = \sum d_i^2/(N - 1),$$

and

$$s = \sqrt{\sum (X_i - \overline{X})^2/(N - 1)} = \sqrt{\sum d_i^2/(N - 1)}.$$

Note that this slight modification will have negligible impact when the number of cases is large. After all, a quotient is about the same whether a numerator is divided by a large number or by that large number less 1. The modification can have a more substantial impact when the number of cases is small, say less than 100 and particularly if less than 60.

Computational formulas for a sample variance are

$$s^2 = [\sum (X_i^2) - (1/N) (\sum X)^2]/(N - 1) = [\sum (X_i^2) - N(\overline{X})^2]/(N - 1).$$

The computational formulas for the standard deviation are just the square roots of those formulas. Once again, the sum of squared values in the formula is not the same as squaring the sum of the values.

A further complication occurs when sampling from a finite population. The formulas given so far assume sampling from an infinite population. However, the population size must be taken into account when sampling from a finite population without replacement (Hays, 1963: 210). If the sample size is denoted as $N$ and the population size as $T$, then the variance is

$$s^2 = [(\sum d_i^2/(N-1)] \times [(T-1)/T] = [\sum d_i^2/(N-1)] \times [1 - (1/T)].$$

The correction factor $1 - (1/T)$ is near 1 except for small populations, so this adjustment has little effect unless the population size is under 100.

*The Variance and Standard Deviation for Grouped Metric Data.* Other versions of the variance and standard deviation formulas can be used when the data are grouped. When working from a frequency distribution in which each value of the variable $X$ is listed along with its corresponding frequency $f$, the population variance can be calculated as

$$\sigma^2 = \sum f_i(X_i - \mu)^2/N = \sum f_i d_i^2/N,$$

or the computational formulas

$$\sigma^2 = [\sum f_i(X_i^2) - (1/N) (\sum f_i X_i)^2]/N = [\sum (f_i X_i^2) - N(\overline{X})^2]/N$$

$$= \sum (f_i X_i^2)/N - \overline{X}^2.$$

The appropriate sample variance formulas are

$$s^2 = \sum f_i(X_i - \overline{X})^2/(N-1) = \sum f_i d_i^2/(N-1),$$

or the computational formulas

$$s^2 = [\sum f_i(X_i^2) - (1/N)(\sum f_i X_i)^2]/(N-1) = [\sum (f_i X_i^2) - N(\overline{X})^2]/(N-1).$$

The standard deviation is the square root of these variance formulas.

When dealing with a continuous variable that has been grouped into classes, the above formulas can be employed with the midpoint of the interval used to represent the interval. Thus, if the true limits of the interval are from 2 to 3, the value 2.5 should be used to represent the interval.

Sometimes it is also necessary to pool variances obtained from different samples. For example, consider combining the variances from separate samples for three different years (say with different numbers of cases for each sample) into an overall variance. If there are $J$ samples and we represent the variance for sample $j$ by $s_j^2$ and the corresponding number of cases as $N_j$, then the *pooled variance* formula is

$$s^2 = \sum [(N_j - 1)\, s_j^2]/(\sum N_j - J).$$

This calculation is illustrated in Table 3.4. If the sample sizes happen to be equal, say $N$, the formula reduces to the average sample variance:

$$s^2 = (N - 1)\,(\sum s_j^2)/(NJ - J) = \sum s_j^2/J.$$

*The Variance and Standard Deviation for Dichotomous Data.* The variance and standard deviations formulas can be further simplified for dichotomous data. The variance of a dichotomous variable (Blalock, 1972: 195) is

$$\sigma^2 = p(1 - p),$$

where $p$ is the proportion of successes. To see this, say that a binary variable is scored 1/0 with $p$ being the proportion of the cases scored 1, so $1 - p$ is the proportion scored 0. According to the computational version of the variance formula, the variance would be

$$\sigma^2 = \sum (X_i^2)/N - (\mu)^2 = \{(N \times p \times 1^2) + [N \times (1 - p) \times 0^2]\}/N - p^2$$

$$= [(Np) + 0]/N - p^2 = p - p^2 = p(1 - p).$$

The standard deviation, of course, is the square root of the variance:[9]

$$\sigma = \sqrt{p\,(1 - p)}\,.$$

Note that the variance is maximal when the proportion $p$ is near one half. Thus, the maximum variance is .25 when $p = .5$, and it diminishes to .16 when $p = .2$ or .8 and to .09 when $p = .1$ or .9.

Gender is a typical example of a dichotomous variable, as it takes on only two possible values: male or female. Say it is scored 0/1, with men coded zero and women coded one. If 53% of the population were women, then the variance for gender would be .53 × .47 = .249.

*Coefficient of Variation.* It is difficult to interpret standard deviation values directly, as what is large depends on the unit in which the variable was measured. For example, is a standard deviation of 100 large or small? It would be large if we were analyzing the weight of people, but it would be small if we were analyzing yearly income values.

The *coefficient of variation* or *coefficient of relative variation* is a statistic that is used to give a better sense of how large a standard deviation is. It divides the standard deviation by the mean of the variable, as shown in the following formula:

$$CV = \sigma/\overline{X}.$$

For example, if a group of people have an average weight of 150 pounds with a standard deviation of 100, the coefficient of variation of weight would be .667. If the average yearly income were $20,000 and the standard deviation were 100, the coefficient of variation of income would be .005. These coefficients of variation can legitimately be compared to find that the weights are more variable than the incomes.

An alternative interpretation of the coefficient of variation is in terms of relative variation. Define the *relative deviation* for observation $i$ as $(X_i - \overline{X})/\overline{X}$. Next, square the coefficient of variation $(\sigma/\overline{X})$. Squaring the standard deviation of a variable divided by its mean gives the variance divided by the mean squared. This can be simplified: $[\Sigma(X_i - \overline{X})^2/N]/\overline{X}^2 = \Sigma[(X_i - \overline{X})/\overline{X}]^2/N$. The latter is just the average of the squared relative deviations $[(X_i - \overline{X})/\overline{X}]^2$. Thus, the squared coefficient of variation equals the average of the squared relative deviations. This is why the coefficient of variation is sometimes called the *coefficient of relative variation.*

*Gini's Mean Difference.* A final measure of spread for metric variables is based on differences rather than deviations. *Gini's mean difference* (Yule & Kendall, 1968: 146-147) is the mean of the absolute value of the differences between all pairs of values:

$$g = \sum |X_i - X_j| \Big/ \binom{N}{2} \qquad \text{summing over } i \leq j$$

$$= \sum |X_i - X_j| / [n(n-1)] \qquad \text{summing over all pairs } i \neq j.$$

Gini's mean difference has intuitive appeal, as it shows the typical difference between a pair of values. For example, in Table 4.1, the mean difference is 7.11, showing that the typical difference in prior convictions between a pair of defendants was 7.11, a value that is close to the standard deviation of 8 but is more readily interpretable. However, it does not generalize beyond the single-variable case in useful ways, so the mean difference is not used often in statistical analysis.

*Summary.* The variance and standard deviation are the most important measures of spread for metric variables. The mean deviation and Gini's mean difference are conceptually simpler, but the variance and standard deviation are the statistics that generalize beyond the single-variable case and that have important mathematical properties.

## Uses of Variance

So far, it has been claimed that the standard deviation and variance are important statistics without showing why. Some of their uses will be described in this section; others will be explained in the next chapter. This discussion is brief and introductory, and is designed mainly to emphasize the widespread use of the variance concept in data analysis and research design.

*Assessing Unusual Values.* One use of the variation on a variable is to assess how unusual any particular value on the variable is. The measure employed for this is called a *standard score* or *Z-score.* If the variable is labelled $X$, the $i$th observation on $X$ is labeled $X_i$, the mean on $X$ is labeled $\mu$, and the standard deviation of $X$ is labeled $\sigma$, then the $Z$-score corresponding to the $i$th observation is

$$Z_i = (X_i - \mu)/\sigma.$$

As an illustration, the standard score for people with 20 previous convictions in the criminal example above is 2.0 if the mean is 4 and the standard deviation is 8. They score 2 standard deviation units above the mean.

The Z-scores on a variable are termed *standardized* because they always have a mean of 0 and a variance of 1. First, consider their mean:

$$\overline{Z} = \sum (Z_i)/N = \sum (X_i - \mu)/(\sigma N) = [1/(\sigma N)]\sum (X_i - \mu) = 0,$$

because the sum of the deviations around the $X$ mean is always 0. Next, consider their variance:

$$s_Z^2 = \sum \{[(X_i - \mu)/\sigma]^2 - 0\}/N = (1/\sigma^2)\sum (X_i - \mu)^2/N = (1/\sigma^2)\sigma^2 = 1.$$

Because standardized variables have a variance of 1, they also have a standard deviation of 1.

Variables are often standardized in statistical analysis to remove some sources of differences between the variables. A typical example would involve constructing an additive index from separate variables. Usually, additive indices are created by just adding up the raw scores on the variables. However, that would be inappropriate if the variables have very different magnitudes or variances (as when constructing a measure of people's status on the basis of the values of their houses and their barbecues) and particularly if they are measured in different units (as when constructing a measure of status based on income in dollars and education in years). In such cases, the variables should be standardized first, and then an index can be created by summing the standardized scores.

What makes standard scores particularly useful is that the laws of statistics and probability provide information on what is an unusual standard score. Z-scores near zero are more likely than values far from zero. According to Chebychev's inequality, regardless of the shape of the distribution of $X$, no more than $(1/k)^2$ proportion of the cases will have standard scores more extreme than $k$. That is,

$$\text{Prob}(|X_i - \overline{X}|/\sigma \geq k) \leq (1/k)^2.$$

For example, the probability that a Z-score's absolute value is greater than or equal to 2 is no more than 1/4.

If the variable has a symmetric distribution, then the probability of a Z-score whose absolute value is greater than or equal to $k$ is no more than $(4/9)(1/k^2)$. That is,

$$\text{Prob}(|X_i - \overline{X}|/\sigma \geq k) \leq (4/9)(1/k)^2.$$

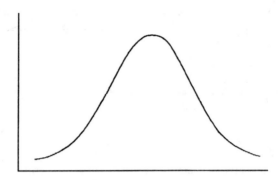

Figure 4.1. Normal Distribution

So, if the variable has a symmetric distribution, the probability of the magnitude of a Z-score being greater than 2 is at most 1/9.

If the variable has the bell-shaped distribution that is called a normal curve (Figure 4.1), then the distribution follows tabulated results. For example, the probability of a Z-score greater than or equal to 1.96 (or less than or equal to −1.96) is .05, versus the 1/4 for values beyond 2 for the more general Chebychev inequality or the 1/9 for a general symmetric distribution. The table showing the likelihood of particular values under a normal curve is included in most statistics texts.

*Assessing the Covariation Between Variables.* Another statistical use of variance involves comparing the variance on two variables to see the extent to which they *covary.* This is usually measured by a *correlation coefficient.* The correlation coefficient used for metric variables is called *Pearson's r,* and it is the average of the products of the standardized values on variables $X$ and $Y$:

$$r = \frac{1}{N} \sum_{i=1}^{N} Z_{X_i} Z_{Y_i}.$$

The values of this statistic range from 0 when there is no covariance between the variables to 1 (or −1) when there is maximal covariance.

Correlations are often examined when assessing causation. Correlation does not in itself prove that one variable "causes" the other. However, finding no correlation between two variables certainly suggests the lack of a causal connection between them. In studying causation, a distinction is made between the *dependent variable,* which is the one being caused, and the *independent variable,* which may be producing the observed differences on the dependent variable. The square of Pearson's $r$ ($r^2$) shows the proportion of the variance of the dependent variable $Y$ that can be accounted for by a linear prediction rule based on the independent variable $X$. For example, a correlation above .7 shows that more than half of the variance in the dependent variable can be accounted for by the independent variable. Thus, correlations are interpreted in terms of variances.

The variance statistic is especially important in analysis of multiple variables, because the variance of the dependent variable can often be decomposed in useful ways. Recall the rule in the previous section that variances (but not standard deviations) are additive when independent results are being summed. This rule is often employed in multivariate analysis, when particular effects can be proven to be independent of one another. The interpretation of Pearson's $r^2$ in the last paragraph was based on this idea, decomposing the variance of the dependent variable into *explained variance* due to a linear relationship with the predictor variable and the remaining *error variance* that cannot be accounted for by linear prediction.

*The Choice of Variables.* Variation is also important to consider at the research-design stage. The simplest lesson is that variation is required in a variable if that variable is to be useful. Say that the determinants of criminal behavior were being studied. A researcher could record the ages of prisoners and use the results to summarize the typical age of criminals. However, without similar data for noncriminals, the study could not be used to check whether criminals are older or younger than the rest of the population. By studying only prisoners, there is no variance on the dependent variable. Variables that lack variation are rarely useful to examine.

Similarly, there must be variation on independent variables. To examine the effects of gender on income, for example, studying only women would not suffice. The interesting part is how men and women differ, because that would allow an examination of the causes of variation between genders. Creating a research design without variance on one of the variables destroys the ability to draw conclusions from the study.

*Sources of Variability.* Why are there differences in scores on a variable? A classification of sources of variability in measurement focuses on the distinction between *true values* and *observed values*. According to this classification, the observed value of a variable is composed of its true value plus an *error* term. That error term can in turn be decomposed into two terms: a *systematic-bias* term and a *random-error* term. Assume that the true values, the systematic bias, and random error are uncorrelated, meaning that the only kind of systematic bias would be a constant added to the true score. The observed variance of a variable then can be decomposed into its true variance and its error variance (because a constant-bias term would lack variance). The random-error term is sometimes further divided into its various sources, such as measurement error, coder error, and sampling error, and each of these errors can have a variance associated with it. Measurement is thus a matter of minimizing particular sources of error variance.

In experimental research, the part of the variance associated with the manipulated variables is considered *systematic variance*, which is to be maximized. The part of the variance associated with other factors is considered *extraneous variance*, which is to be controlled as by random assignment of subjects to different experimental groups. The remaining variance due to random fluctuations is considered *error variance*, which is to be minimized by controlling experimental conditions or by increasing the reliability of the measures. This classification leads to the suggestion by Kerlinger (1973) in his research-design textbook that the researcher should "maximize systematic variance, control extraneous variance, and minimize error variance." Thus, research design itself can be considered an exercise in variance control. All in all, the variance concept is of critical importance in research design as well as in data analysis.

## Order-Based Measures of Spread

The concept of spread is also applicable to ordinal data, though spread is rarely measured at a purely ordinal level. Measures of spread for ordinal data will be described in this section, along with measures that are based on the order of numeric values. The major measures of spread discussed in this section are the range and, especially, the interquartile range (IQR).

*Range.* The simplest order-based measure of spread is the range of values: the difference between the largest and smallest data values.

Let $X_{max}$ represent the largest data value and $X_{min}$ denote the smallest data value, so

$$\text{Range} = X_{max} - X_{min}.$$

The range indicates how much the variable varies in practice. Its minimum value is zero when there is no spread on the variable.

As an example, say that we counted the number of prior convictions of 10 criminal defendants. If each defendant had exactly 4 prior convictions, the range would be 0. The range would be 20 if the numbers of prior convictions went from a maximum of 20 down to a minimum of 0.

The main advantage of the range as a measure of spread is its ease of calculation. However, it is very much affected by extreme values, even if they are not atypical. For example, if nine defendants had no prior convictions and the remaining defendant had 20, the range would be 20 because of the single outlier. As a result, the range is considered to be a nonresistant measure of spread. More resistant measures are generally preferred.

*Interquartile Range and Variants.* This sensitivity of the range to extreme cases is sometimes remedied by switching to such variants as the *interquartile range* (also known in the EDA literature as the *midspread, H-spread,* or *F-spread*). For this measure, determine what data value corresponds to the 75th percentile of cases ($Q_3$: the upper quartile) and what data value corresponds to the 25th percentile ($Q_1$: the lower quartile). The IQR is the difference between those values:

$$\text{IQR} = Q_3 - Q_1.$$

By lopping off the extreme cases, the IQR is less sensitive to outliers than is the full range, so it is a more resistant measure of spread.

As described in Chapter 1, exploratory data analysis emphasizes becoming familiar with the data at an intuitive level. Also, EDA emphasizes the use of resistant statistics. The IQR is a statistic favored in EDA, because it is intuitive, resistant, and has desirable properties over a variety of different distributions for the variable (Iglewicz, 1983).

The limitation of the IQR is that there is an ad hoc quality to its calculation, because there is nothing magical about the 75th and 25th percentiles. Indeed, some EDA advocates would suggest computing a variety of IQR-like statistics, such as the difference between the top and bottom eighths of the distribution, and so on. This multiplicity of possible ranges serves as a reminder that EDA-based statistics are intended for exploration of a set of data more than as final summary statistics.

Several variants of the IQR also have been proposed as measures of spread. The *quartile deviation* (QD); (also *semi-interquartile range* or *quartile range*) is the interquartile range divided by 2:

$$QD = (Q_3 - Q_1)/2.$$

The division by 2 is intended to give the statistic the feel of a typical deviation from the center, here how much the quartiles typically deviate from the median. The QD also can be thought of as the average of the range from the 25th percentile to the 50th percentile and the range from the 50th percentile to the 75th percentile.

The interquartile range and related ranges have a zero value when there is no spread on the variable. Their values are unlimited as the spread on the variable increases. The IQR is fairly easy to compute, but it does not lead to useful generalizations beyond the single-variable case.

The interpretation of the size of range-based spread coefficients depends on the units in which the variables are measured. Following the coefficient of variation logic, a normed version can be obtained by dividing the spread statistic by a measure of center. The *coefficient of quartile variation* (CQV) is the interquartile difference divided by the sum of the first and third quartiles (Leabo, 1972: 110):

$$CQV = (Q_3 - Q_1)/(Q_3 + Q_1).$$

This statistic equals the quartile deviation divided by the midhinge (defined in Chapter 3), which emphasizes its use of coefficient of variation logic.

*Box Plots.* One of the most inventive developments in statistics in recent years has been the creation of new graphic procedures for data exploration. In particular, *box plots* (also known as *box-and-whisker diagrams*) have been devised for displaying the ordinal distribution of variables. The box plot simultaneously shows the median of a variable, its range, and its interquartile range, and emphasizes which observations are outliers. Thus, box plots give a quick view of both center and spread.

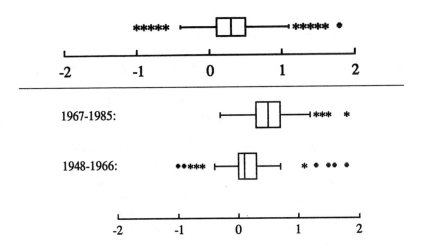

Figure 4.2. Section A. Monthly Inflation Rates, 1948-1985
Section B. Monthly Inflation Rates, by Years

Figure 4.2, section a, shows the box plot corresponding to the monthly inflation rates for the U.S. economy from 1948 through 1985. The horizontal axis shows the values of the variable, from ⁻2 through +2. Note the three vertical lines in the plot. The middle one represents the median, showing that the median for these data is roughly 0.3. The other two vertical bars show the first quartile (about .1) and third quartile (about .5). There is a box around these three vertical lines; the horizontal width of this box represents the interquartile range. Beyond the interquartile range, values within 1.5 times the midspread (interquartile range) of the first or third quartiles are shown and are connected to the main box with lines, colorfully termed *whiskers*. Outliers between 1.5 and 3 times the interquartile range from the first or third quartiles (said to be outside the *inner fences*) are plotted with stars. Extreme outliers more than 3 times the interquartile range from the first or third quartiles (said to be outside the *outer fences*) are plotted as filled circles.

Box plots are particularly useful when comparing the distribution of the same variable for different subgroups of observations. Figure 4.2, section b, shows box plots for inflation for 1948-1966 and 1967-1985 separately. The median inflation rate is seen to be higher in the later period. Also, the interquartile range was larger in the later period, though the earlier period experienced more atypical monthly values. The subgroup differences are apparent from a glance at these plots. Comparing different box plots can highlight differences in medians, quartiles, spreads, and/or outliers.

The remaining measures in this chapter are used less often, so some readers might want to skip ahead to the next chapter at this point.

*Absolute Deviations From the Median.* Additional possible order-based measure of spread are based on the absolute deviations from the median. Let the deviation $d_i$ be defined as the arithmetic difference between the value for an observation $X_i$ and the median, $d_i = X_i - X_{median}$, and let the absolute deviation $|d_i| = |X_i - X_{median}|$. The *average deviation from the median* is the average of these absolute deviations:

$$AD = \sum |X_i - X_{median}|/N.$$

As an example, the median for Table 4.1 is 0, the absolute deviations from that median sum to 40, and the number of cases is 10, so the average deviation from the median is 4. The average deviation from the median is minimal compared to the mean deviation from any other possible measure of center (Yule & Kendall, 1968: 138).

A dispersion measure used in the EDA approach is the *median absolute deviation*, the median of the deviations defined above:

$$MAD = median_i |X_i - X_{median}|.$$

The median absolute deviation for Table 4.1 is 0. EDA work suggests that the MAD has desirable properties over a variety of distributions for the variable (Iglewicz, 1983).

Just as the coefficient of variation is the standard deviation normed by dividing through by the mean, the *coefficient of dispersion* (CD) is the average absolute deviation from the median normed by dividing through by the median:

$$CD = \sum |X_i - X_{median}|/(NX_{median}).$$

This is a spread measure that corrects for the magnitude of the variable.

Although these measures have some desirable properties, absolute values are awkward to manipulate algebraically. Because of this, these measures do not lead to useful generalizations when we move into statistics for more than one variable. As a result, these measures of spread are rarely used.

*Leik's D.* The purest ordinal measure of spread was developed by Leik (1966) in his study of consensus (Rae & Taylor, 1970: 125-127). First, assume that the variable has been placed in its proper order. Denote the proportions of the observations in each of the $K$ different categories as $p_1$, $p_2, \ldots, p_K$. Define the cumulative proportion for category $k$ as $c_k = \Sigma p_j$ for $j \leq k$. Then let the difference $d_k = c_k$ if $c_k \leq 0.5$ and $1 - c_k$ otherwise. Leik proposes as a measure of dispersion:

$$D = 2\sum d_k/(K - 1).$$

As an example, say that there are four individuals and three categories, with one person in the first category, two in the middle category, and one in the last category (see Table 4.3, section a). The cumulative proportions for the three categories are $c_1 = 0.25$, $c_2 = 0.75$, and $c_3 = 1.00$. The corresponding differences are $d_1 = 0.25$, $d_2 = 0.25$, and $d_3 = 0$. Leik's $D = 2(0.25 + 0.25 + 0.00)/(3 - 1) = 2 \times 0.50/2 = 0.50$. This statistic is zero if there is no dispersion: if all people fall in the same category (section b). Maximum dispersion occurs when the cases are polarized, with half at each extreme, in which case $D$ takes on a maximal value of 1 (section c).

Leik's $D$ logic is fully appropriate for ordinal data, without requiring a conversion to numeric scores, but it is used infrequently.

*Summary.* There are several order-based measures of spread. The range is too nonresistant to be useful. The interquartile range and median average deviation have some useful properties, but they do not generalize to more than one variable. Leik's $D$ is very purely ordinal, but it is rarely used. Putting these considerations together, order-based measures of spread are limited in their value. As a result, the variance and standard deviation are frequently employed even on ordinal data.

## Frequency-Based Measures of Spread

Spread can be measured for nominal variables in terms of the degree of heterogeneity on the variable. Zero spread denotes complete homogeneity (all cases falling in the same category), whereas higher values indicate greater heterogeneity. Spread measures for nominal variables are based on the frequencies of the categories. In reading

TABLE 4.3
Examples for Illustrating Leik's D

| | Section A. Calculation of Leik's D | | | |
| | Category 1 | Category 2 | Category 3 | Sum |
|---|---|---|---|---|
| Frequency | 1 | 2 | 1 | 4 |
| Proportion | .25 | .50 | .25 | 1.00 |
| Cumulative proportion | .25 | .75 | 1.00 | |
| Difference | .25 | .25 | .00 | .50 |
| $D = 2 \times 0.5/(3 - 1) = 2 \times 0.5/2 = 0.5$ | | | | |

| | Section B. No Dispersion | | | |
| | Category 1 | Category 2 | Category 3 | Sum |
|---|---|---|---|---|
| Frequency | 0 | 4 | 0 | 4 |
| Proportion | .00 | 1.00 | .00 | 1.00 |
| Cumulative proportion | .00 | 1.00 | 1.00 | |
| Difference | .00 | .00 | .00 | .00 |
| $D = 2 \times 0/(3 - 1) = 0$ | | | | |

| | Section C. Maximal Dispersion | | | |
| | Category 1 | Category 2 | Category 3 | Sum |
|---|---|---|---|---|
| Frequency | 2 | 0 | 2 | 4 |
| Proportion | .50 | .00 | .50 | 1.00 |
| Cumulative proportion | .50 | .50 | 1.00 | |
| Difference | .50 | .50 | .00 | 1.00 |
| $D = 2 \times 1/(3 - 1) = 2 \times 1/2 = 2/2 = 1.00$ | | | | |

this section, it should be kept in mind that there is no single agreed-upon measure of spread for nominal data.

*Variation Ratio.* The simplest measure of spread for nominal data is called the *variation ratio*. It is just the proportion of cases that do not fall into the modal category

$$\text{Variation Ratio} = 1 - (f_{mode}/N),$$

where $f$ stands for frequency, $f_{mode}$ is the frequency of the modal category, and $N$ is the total number of cases. This is a useful measure of spread because it shows how descriptive the mode is of the data.

TABLE 4.4
Distributions of Religions

| Religion | Actual | Unanimity | Polarized | Individuality | Uniform |
|----------|--------|-----------|-----------|---------------|---------|
| Protestant | 80 | 6 | 3 | 1 | 2 |
| Catholic | 60 | 0 | 3 | 1 | 2 |
| Jewish | 10 | 0 | 0 | 1 | 2 |
| Muslim | — | 0 | 0 | 1 | 0 |
| Other | 20 | 0 | 0 | 1 | 0 |
| None | 30 | 0 | 0 | 1 | 0 |
| Total | 200 | 6 | 6 | 6 | 6 |
| | | | | | |
| Mode | Protestant | Protestant | not unique | not unique | not unique |
| | | | | | |
| Variation ratio | .600 | .00 | .50 | .83 | .67 |
| Index of diversity | .715 | .00 | .50 | .83 | .67 |
| IQV | .894 | .00 | 1.00 | 1.00 | 1.00 |
| Entropy | 2.009 | .00 | 1.00 | 2.58 | 1.58 |
| Standardized entropy | .865 | .00 | 1.00 | 1.00 | 1.00 |

For an example of the variation ratio, look at data on religious affiliations in Table 4.4. The modal religion for column 2 is Protestant, with 40% of the sample being Protestant; the variation ratio is .60.

The variation ratio would be zero if all cases fell into the same category. Its maximal value depends on the number of categories of the variable. If there are $K$ categories and each occurs equally with frequency $N/K$ (a uniform distribution), then the variation ratio is $1 - (1/K)$, which approaches 1 as the number of categories $K$ becomes infinitely large. Thus, it is maximal under individuality—when each case is in a separate category.

The variation ratio is simple to compute, but it has the disadvantage of being based only on the proportion of cases in the modal category. Other measures of nominal spread take the full distribution of cases into account.

*Index of Diversity.* A second measure of spread for nominal variables is the *index of diversity, D.* This is a dispersion measure based on the proportion of cases in each category. It squares each of those proportions, sums the squares, and subtracts the sum of squares from 1:

$$D = 1 - p_1^2 - p_2^2 - \ldots - p_K^2 = 1 - \sum_k p_k^2,$$

where $p_k$ is the proportion of cases in category $k$, $K$ is the number of categories, and $\Sigma$ stands for summation—the summation of the $p_k^2$ terms for each category. This index shows the degree of *concentration* of the cases in a few large categories, because squaring proportions emphasizes the large proportions much more than small ones (Coulter, 1984).

In the religions example (Table 4.4), with 40% Protestant, 30% Catholic, 5% Jewish, 10% other, and 15% none, the sum of squared proportions is $.16 + .09 + .0025 + .01 + .0225 = .285$, so $D$ is $1 - .285 = .715$.

The index of diversity has been developed independently in many fields as a measure of heterogeneity. For example, it is the same as the fractionalization measure developed by Taylor and Hudson (1972: 216; also Waldman, 1976) to summarize the spread between the numbers of votes received by political parties in multiparty elections.

The index of diversity approaches zero if nearly all cases fall into the same category. It is maximal under individuality—when each case is in a separate category. However, its maximum value depends on the number of categories, so $D$ values cannot be compared across distributions with differing numbers of categories. If there were $K$ categories, with an equal proportion of cases in each category, $D$ would have the maximum value of $(K - 1)/K$. Thus in the religions example, the maximum diversity is .80 (= 4/5), because there are five religious groups. What makes this unusual is that the maximum would increase if there were more categories. For example, if we subdivided the Protestant category into Baptist, Presbyterian, Methodist, Lutheran, and other Protestants, we would have 10 categories, with a maximum diversity of .90 (= 9/10). For many purposes, it would be more useful were the diversity index normed to go from 0 to 1 regardless of the number of categories.

*Index of Qualitative Variation.* A third measure of spread for nominal variables, the *index of qualitative variation* (IQV), norms the diversity index so that the value of 1 always represents maximum spread. To do this, it simply divides the index of diversity by its maximum for the actual number of categories: $(K - 1)/K$. The formula is

$$\text{IQV} = (1 - p_1^2 - p_2^2 - \ldots - p_K^2]/[(K - 1)/K].$$

In the religions example of Table 4.4, with five religious categories the index of qualitative variation is $.715/.80 = .894$. This high IQV indicates that there is considerable dispersion across religions in this sample. It is 0 when all cases fall into a single category, and 1 under uniformity, when the cases are evenly spread across the $K$ categories.

Which nominal measure of spread is more useful depends partly on how we define nominal spread. Say we were comparing party competition in two nations: a two-party system in which each party won 50% of the vote and a multiparty system in which each of 10 parties obtained an equal 10% share of the vote. The IQV value would be 1.00 in each case, because the diversity is maximal given the number of categories. Yet there is a real sense in which there is more dispersion in the 10-party case than in the two-party system. If we felt this dispersion was important to capture, we would have to return to the index of diversity, where we would find a value of .90 for the 10-party nation versus a value of .50 for the two-party system. Thus, correction for the number of categories would be inappropriate when the existence of more categories in itself signifies greater diversity.

*Entropy.* A fourth measure of spread for nominal variables is based on information theory (Krippendorff, 1986). Information-theory-based statistics gauge how much information is conveyed by a distribution. There is no uncertainty when all cases fall in the same category. The greater the spread of cases across categories, the more uncertainty.

Independent bits of information are counted. By definition, there is exactly one bit of uncertainty in a choice between two equal alternatives. Less uncertainty would exist if one alternative were more popular than the other. An even choice among two alternatives provides one bit of uncertainty, an even choice among four alternatives (two-squared) provides two bits of uncertainty, an even choice among eight alternatives (two-cubed) provides three bits, and so on. Thus, the number of independent bits of information can be calculated by taking the logarithm to the base 2 of the number of alternatives, adjusted for their differential popularities.

*Entropy* (or *uncertainty*) is measured by looking at the proportion of cases in each category $k$. This proportion is multiplied by the negative[10] of its logarithm (usually to the base 2), which gives $-p_k\log_2(p_k)$. The uncertainty of a distribution is defined as the sum of this value over all categories:

$$H'(X) = - \sum_k p_k \log_2(p_k) = - 3.3219 \sum_k p_k \log_{10}(p_k).$$

72

The second version of the formula states entropy in terms of common logs to the base 10.

In the religions example of Table 4.4, the entropy is 2.009. This can be interpreted as saying that the spread among the religious categories is approximately that of choosing between four equally prevalent religions.

There is no uncertainty when all observations are in the same category. In that case, $p_1 = 1$. By definition, the logarithm of 1 is 0, so the entropy value for this situation is zero. By contrast, if there is a uniform distribution across $K$ categories, then entropy equals $-\Sigma(1/K)\log_2(1/K) = -K(1/K)[\log_2(1) - \log_2(K)] = -[0 - \log_2(K)] = \log_2(K)$. In other words, the more categories, the greater the uncertainty. Its maximum value thus depends on the number of categories, with the greatest value under individuality.

The entropy statistic can be normed so its maximum is 1 regardless of the number of categories of the variable. The entropy formula can be modified to have this characteristic by dividing through by its maximum value to obtain what is termed *standardized entropy*:[11]

$$J' = -\sum_k p_k \log(p_k) / \log(K).$$

In the religions example, the standardized entropy is .865.

Entropy statistics are little used because logs to the base 2 are awkward to compute and because most researchers are uncomfortable with logarithms. However, the theoretical basis of these statistics is very strong. Other nominal measures of spread have an ad hoc basis to them, whereas entropy statistics are elegantly based on information theory. A further advantage is that entropy statistics generalize readily to multiple variables, so uncertainty-based measures of association between two variables can be used to determine how much an explanatory variable helps reduce the uncertainty as to the dependent-variable category in which a case belongs.

*Other Measures.* Several other measures of spread for nominal variables have been devised, usually by researchers solving their own substantive problems. Thus, political scientists developed several measures of the dispersion of the seat totals won by different parties in multiparty legislatures (Waldman, 1976). A typical example is Rae and Taylor's (1970) *fragmentation* statistic, which is the proportion of pairs of cases that are not in the same category; it approximately equals the index of diversity for large numbers of cases. Similarly, biologists constructed several *indices of ecological diversity* (Kotz, Johnson, & Read, 1983, vol. 2: 409), where the existence of a large number of species nearly equal in size is considered high diversity. Also, several disciplines developed measures of *equality* (Coulter, 1984) or integration, such as $1 - \Sigma |p_k - (1/K)|$, which is based on the difference between proportional shares and the average proportional share.

*Summary.* There is no common agreement as to which frequency-based measure of spread is best. Indeed, computer programs rarely provide *any* of them. Each has a value of zero when all cases are in the same category. The greater the heterogeneity of the observations, the higher the value for these statistics. As shown in the last four columns of Table 4.4, they differ in their maximal values. The index of qualitative variation and standardized entropy have maximum values of 1 when the distribution is uniform; the others are maximal when each case is in a separate category, with their maximum value depending on the number of categories.

## Discussion

*Comparisons of Measures of Spread.* Spread measures all accept the same definition of zero variation, but they use different interpretations of maximum spread (see Table 4.5). The metric and order-based measures are maximal when the variable is polarized, with half of the cases at the maximum value and the other half at the minimum. The frequency-based measures instead are maximal when there is a uniform distribution of cases across the categories, or when there are as many categories as observations. Also, some spread measures are normed, either to have a maximum value of 1 or by dividing through by a central-tendency value to control for the unit in which the variable is measured. Normed values are generally more interpretable, although raw values may be purer measures of spread.

Table 4.6 compares the major measures of spread described in this chapter along the desirable criteria for descriptive statistics listed in Chapter 1. Some of the evaluations in the table are debatable, but they give a useful beginning point for considering the statistics. The advantages of the standard deviation (and variance) are that they are

TABLE 4.5
Maximum Value Conditions for Measures of Spread

| Measure | Maximum Value | Maximum Condition for Fixed # of Cases | Maximum Dependent on # Categories | Normed |
|---|---|---|---|---|
| Mean deviation | unlimited | polarized | no | no |
| Variance | unlimited | polarized | no | no |
| Standard deviation | unlimited | polarized | no | no |
| Coefficient of variation | unlimited | | no | yes |
| Gini's mean difference | unlimited | polarized | no | no |
| Range | unlimited | | no | no |
| Interquartile range | unlimited | polarized | no | no |
| Quartile deviation | unlimited | polarized | no | no |
| Coefficient of quartile variation | unlimited | | no | yes |
| Median absolute deviation | unlimited | polarized | no | no |
| Coefficient of dispersion | unlimited | | no | yes |
| Leik's $D$ | 1 | polarized | yes | no |
| Variation ratio | $\rightarrow 1$ | individuality | yes | no |
| Index of diversity | $\rightarrow 1$ | individuality | yes | no |
| Index of qualitative variation | 1 | uniformity | no | 0-1 |
| Entropy | unlimited | individuality | yes | no |
| Standardized entropy | 1 | uniformity | no | 0-1 |

algebraic, stable under sampling, and generalizable to two or more variables. The interquartile range is easier to understand and to calculate, more resistant to outliers, and can often be computed for open-ended variables. The frequency-based measures generally do not excel on the criteria, but they are appropriate for nominal data. Rather than choose a single measure of spread, often it is more appropriate to use several of these measures together to highlight different aspects of the dispersion.

The values of these measures of spread can be compared for some known distributions. In particular, say that the variable has a normal distribution, the bell-shaped distribution shown in Figure 4.1. This distribution has well-known mathematical properties that have been extensively studied over the years. For such a distribution, the interquartile range is 1.349 times the standard deviation (Velleman & Hoaglin, 1981: 54), and the mean deviation is .7979 times the standard deviation (Leabo, 1972: 114). This suggests that the standard devia-

TABLE 4.6
Properties of Measures of Spread

| Property | Index of Diversity | Interquartile Range | Standard Deviation |
|---|---|---|---|
| Level of measurement | nominal or higher | ordinal or higher | metric (usually) |
| Rigidly defined | yes | yes | yes |
| Based on all cases | yes | yes | yes |
| Simple to understand | medium | yes | no |
| Easy to calculate | yes | yes | medium |
| Algebraic | yes | no | yes |
| Stable under sampling | unknown | unknown | yes |
| Single valued | yes | yes | yes |
| Resistant to outliers | yes | yes | no |
| Generalize to two-variable statistics | no | no | yes |
| Insensitive to combining categories | no | yes | yes |
| Computed for open-ended variables | no | yes | no |
| In same units as data values | no | yes | yes |

tion will generally be larger than the average unsigned deviation from the mean (as measured by the mean deviation) and smaller than the interquartile range. These values could differ considerably for other distributions, although the 1.349 value for the interquartile range should not be terribly sensitive to the exact distribution because the measure is based on quartiles.

*Mathematical Properties of Measures of Spread.* A measure of spread should have two mathematical properties when applied to metric data. First, if a constant $k$ is added to every value on the variable, the spread statistic should remain unchanged. Adding the constant changes the location of the values, but not the spread between them. Second, if a multiplier $m$ is multiplied by every value of the variable, the spread then should be multiplied by the absolute value of $m$. Putting these two points together, the measure of spread on a variable transformed in a linear fashion should be

$$\text{Spread } (k + mX_i) = |m| \times \text{Spread}(X_i).$$

The range, interquartile range, mean deviation, and standard deviation all satisfy these conditions. Linear transformations of the data values increase these measures of spread in a multiplicative fashion. Consider, for example, a variable measured on a scale of 0 to 100, with 50 as neutral point. If a researcher wanted to convert this variable to a -100 to 100 scale, with 0 as neutral point, the conversion rule would be $2X - 100$, so the spread would double. Notice that the variance does not satisfy these conditions; its value would be multiplied by $m^2$, the square of the multiplier.

*Summary.* The most common measures of dispersion for metric data are the variance and its unsquared cousin, the standard deviation. These two measures must be understood well if the statistics of relationships between two or more variables are to be comprehended. Dispersion measures exist for other types of data, some (particularly the interquartile range) based on order-properties of the data and others based on the frequencies of the categories. Most of these measures do not generalize well beyond one variable, but they are effective in gauging the amount of dispersion when the variable is nonmetric.

## 5. CENTER AND SPREAD IN SAMPLES

Measures of center and spread have been presented in Chapters 3 and 4 from the *descriptive* point of view, showing how to summarize the results for the observed cases. An alternative *inferential* perspective is to use the *sample* of cases to describe a larger *population* of interest.

Often the researcher is interested in determining the value of a population *parameter*, such as a mean for the population. By convention, population parameters are denoted by Greek letters, such as mu ($\mu$) for the population mean and sigma ($\sigma$) for the standard deviation. A sample does not permit the researcher to view the value of the population parameter directly. Instead, it permits the researcher to compute a sample *statistic,* such as the mean for the sample. These sample statistics are denoted by italic (Latin) letters, such as $\overline{X}$ for the sample mean and $s$ for the standard deviation. Even when computing sample statistics, researchers generally are more interested in estimating the population parameters.

This chapter will introduce the estimation of center and spread for samples. In doing so, the importance of the variance statistic in classic statistics will be emphasized further.

## Sampling Distributions

In addition to the distribution of the variable for the sample and the distribution of the variable for the population, a third distribution is of interest. It is called a *sampling distribution*. Imagine taking an infinite series of random samples of a given size and computing the variable's mean for each sample. The distribution of those sample means is known as the *sampling distribution of means*. Of course only one sample is taken in research applications, but this hypothetical distribution of sample means is important in statistical theory. Statistical inference is based on this sampling distribution; its variation and shape must be determined before statistical inference can be explained.

*Standard Error of the Mean.* The computational formula for the variance presented in Chapter 4 can be applied to obtain the variance of this sampling distribution of means:

$$\sigma_{\bar{X}}^2 = \sigma^2/N.$$

This formula can be derived by applying the formula for the variance of a weighted sum of independent results: $\text{Var}(cA + dB) = c^2\text{var}(A) + d^2\text{var}(B)$, where $c$ and $d$ are constants and $A$ and $B$ are independent results. When a sample of $N$ independent observations is taken, the mean $\bar{X}$ can be expressed as $(1/N)X_1 + (1/N)X_2 + \ldots + (1/N)X_N$. Applying the weighted rule above, the variance of sample means must then be $(1/N^2)\text{Var}(X) + (1/N^2)\text{Var}(X) + \ldots + (1/N^2)\text{Var}(X) = N[(1/N^2)\text{Var}(X)] = \text{Var}(X)/N = \sigma^2/N$.

The *standard error of the mean* is defined to be the standard deviation of the sampling distribution of means—the standard deviation of the means of the several samples. It is the square root of the variance of the mean just defined. This standard error equals the population standard deviation divided by the square root of the number of cases:

$$s_\text{m} = \sigma/\sqrt{N}.$$

When using an estimated sample standard deviation, the estimated standard error for the mean is

$$\text{est } s_m = s/\sqrt{N} = \sqrt{\sum (X_i - \overline{X})^2/N(N-1)} \; .$$

The standard error is an important measure when using sample data to make inferences about populations, as will be shown shortly.

A correction factor is necessary when sampling from a finite population without replacement. If the sample size is $N$ and the population size is $T$, then the estimated standard error of the mean is

$$\text{est } s_m = s/\sqrt{N} \times \sqrt{1 - (N/T)} \; .$$

When the sampling fraction $N/T$ is small, as in most samples where less than 1% of the total population is being sampled, the multiplier $\sqrt{1 - (N/T)}$ is near 1 and does not have much effect on the standard error. This correction becomes more important when a large fraction of the population is sampled. For example, if half of the population is sampled, then the multiplier is about .7, so the standard error is 30% lower than it would otherwise be for a sample of that size.

Similarly, the standard error of a proportion is its standard deviation divided by the square root of the number of cases:

$$s_p = \sqrt{p(1-p)/N} \; ,$$

or, when sampling without replacement from a finite population of size $T$,

$$s_p = \sqrt{p(1-p)/(N-1)} \times \sqrt{1 - (N/T)} \; .$$

Again, that last term is a correction factor that has little effect unless a large fraction of the total population is being sampled. The use of this standard error for a proportion in polling is described below.

*Central-Limit Theorem.* Most variables do not have the normal distribution that was shown in Figure 4.1. However, that distribution is vital in statistics because of an important theorem. The theorem involves the sampling distribution of the mean—the distribution of means that would be obtained if a large number of samples were taken and the mean was computed for each of these samples. According to the *central-limit theorem,* for large sample sizes the sampling distribution of the mean $\overline{X}$ is approximately normal, with mean equal to the population mean $\mu$ and standard deviation equal to the standard error just defined.

The central-limit theorem holds regardless of the shape of the variable's distribution (so long as it has a finite standard deviation), so that the mean of a variable can be considered to have a normal distribution even if the variable itself does not. As a result, the normal distribution can be used to assess the statistical significance of sample means.

## Statistical Inference

Statistical tests about the mean can be conducted by putting together the various results already obtained.

Recall from the discussion of standard scores in Chapter 4 that when a variable has a normal distribution, the probability of a $Z$-score greater than or equal to 1.96 (or less than or equal to $-1.96$) is .05. We have just seen that the sample mean $\overline{X}$ has a normal distribution with mean $\mu$ and standard deviation $s_m$. Define the *test statistic* as the $Z$-score for $\overline{X}$: $|\overline{X} - \mu|/s_m$. The probability of a test statistic greater than or equal to 1.96 by chance alone is .05. That is,

$$\text{Prob}(|\overline{X} - \mu|/s_m \geq 1.96) \leq .05.$$

Therefore, there is only a .05 chance of a sample mean being more than 1.96 standard errors from the population mean.

To see how significance testing works, say that we want to test whether the population mean on a variable equals some value, such as 100. Say also that a particular sample of 64 cases gives a mean of 125 with a standard deviation of 120, which translates to an estimated standard error of $120/\sqrt{64} = 120/8 = 15$. The statistical question then is whether it is likely that we would have a sample 25 points away from the hypothesized population mean of 100 with a standard error this size.

The test is conducted by computing the test statistic $|\overline{X} - \mu|/s_m$. If the test statistic is at least 1.96, then we can conclude with considerable confidence that the population mean does not equal the hypothesized value of 100; if the test statistic is less than 1.96, then we cannot reject the hypothesis that the true mean equals 100. The test statistic $|\bar{X} - \mu|/s_m = |125 - 100|/15 = 25/15 = 1.667$, which is less than 1.96. As a result, the sample mean 125 would not be considered statistically different from the hypothesized population mean of 100 at the .05 level of significance. With a sample of only 64 cases, we could have a sample mean of 125 even if the population mean were 100. On the other hand, were our sample mean 145, we would reject the hypothesis that the true mean is 100.

Significance tests for proportions are similar. As indicated above, the standard error of a proportion is $\sqrt{p(1-p)/N}$. So to test whether a sample proportion $p$ significantly differs from .50, for example, the test statistic would be $|p - .50|/\sqrt{p(1-p)/N}$. The possibility that the true population proportion is .50 could be rejected at the .05 level of significance if this test statistic is greater than 2 (or, more precisely, 1.96).

In public-opinion polling, it is more common to use sample surveys to try to estimate population proportions. Say that a *simple random sample* is taken, each element having the same chance of being included in the sample. In that case, the *sampling error* usually is defined as

$$se = 1.96\sqrt{p(1-p)/(N-1)} \, ,$$

which is maximal when $p = .50$. This simplifies to a maximum sampling error of *roughly* $1/\sqrt{N}$. Thus, 95% of proportions estimated from simple random samples of size 900 should be within 3.33% (= $1/\sqrt{900}$) of the true population proportion. If a sample survey of 900 people finds that 60% favor a particular policy, it really is showing that 60% ± 3.33% = 56.67% – 63.33% of the larger population probably favor that policy.

Other significance tests are used for testing whether there is a significant difference between two means, for the size of a variance (a *chi-square* test), and for whether one variable has a greater variance than another (an *F* test). These tests are beyond the scope of this book.

*Summary.* When dealing with metric variables, it is possible to make statistical inferences about the center and spread for the population of interest based on sample statistics. For example, the sampling distribution of the mean has a normal distribution, centered around the true population mean and with a standard deviation corresponding to the estimated standard deviation of the variable divided by the square root of the number of cases. As a result, 95% of the sample means will be within approximately two standard-error units of the true population mean. This permits testing of statistical hypotheses regarding whether a sample mean is compatible with a hypothesized value of the population mean. Significance tests have been developed for some ordinal and nominal measures of center and spread, but they are too specialized to present here.

## Appendix: Technical Properties of Estimators

Statisticians have defined several technical properties of estimators by which to evaluate how well sample statistics, such as $\overline{X}$, estimate population parameters, such as $\mu$. These properties were not mentioned in Chapters 3 and 4 because of their complexity, though the basic points are easy to follow.

The first technical property is called *consistency*. According to this criterion, as the sample size $N$ becomes larger, the sample statistic should approximate the population parameter more closely. This criterion is stated in terms of the difference between those two values:

$$\text{Prob}(|\text{sample statistic} - \text{population parameter}| < \delta) \to 1 \text{ as } N \to \infty,$$

regardless of the value of $\delta$ (delta). The arrows in this equation are read as "approaches," so the condition is that the probability that the difference between the sample statistic and population parameter becomes arbitrarily small approaches certainty as the number of cases approaches infinity.

Consistency also can be stated in terms of the expected value of the square of the difference between the sample statistic and the population parameter: This expected value should approach zero as the number of cases approaches infinity. An *expected value* is similar to a mean—if the statistical operation were performed several times and then the average of the results were taken, that is the expected value. More technically, an expected value is a weighted mean, where each value is weighted by its probability:

$$E(X) = \sum x p_x, \qquad \text{summed over all possible values of } X.$$

Consistency implies that

$$E(\text{sample statistic} - \text{population parameter})^2 \to 0 \text{ as } N \to \infty.$$

Some texts use that as the definition of consistency. Whether an estimator is consistent can be determined only by a mathematical proof.

The sample mean is a consistent estimator of the population mean:

$$\text{Prob}(|\overline{X} - \mu| < \delta) \to 1 \text{ as } N \to \infty.$$

Although that may not be surprising, for a symmetric population distribution the sample median is also a consistent estimator of the population mean:

$$\text{Prob}(|X_{\text{median}} - \mu| < \delta) \to 1 \text{ as } N \to \infty.$$

If many large samples were taken, the average difference between the sample median and the population mean would approach 0. Incidentally, the sample variance is a consistent estimator of the population variance:

$$\text{Prob}(|s^2 - \sigma^2| < \delta) \to 1 \text{ as } N \to \infty.$$

Consistency is a large-sample property—it describes the behavior of the sample statistic as the sample size is made very large. An inconsistent statistic is a poor choice, even for large samples. However, consistency does not guarantee that a statistic is useful for small samples. The remaining properties to be discussed involve properties of estimators for small samples.

An estimator should also be *unbiased*. An unbiased sample statistic has as its expected value the population parameter being estimated:

$$E(\text{sample statistic}) = \text{population parameter}.$$

An expected value is an average, so this says that if several samples are taken, the sample statistic is calculated on each, and these several sample statistics are averaged, then that average should equal the population parameter. Bias can be determined only by mathematical proof.

The sample mean is an unbiased estimator of the population mean: $E(\overline{X}) = \mu$. To see this, substitute on the left-hand side the formula for the mean:

$$E(\sum X_i/N) = E(\sum X_i)/N = \sum E(X_i)/N = (N\mu)/N = \mu.$$

Although the sample median is a consistent estimator of the population mean for symmetric distributions, that estimate is biased: $E(X_{\text{median}}) \neq \mu$. The sample mean is the preferred estimator of the mean because it is not biased.

A more surprising result is that applying the formula for the population variance to sample data leads to biased estimation. Let $\sigma^2$ represent the true population variance, and define $s_X^2 = \Sigma(X_i - \overline{X})^2/N$, or the computational equivalent: $(\Sigma X_i^2)/N - \overline{X}^2$. When the $s_X^2$ formula is applied to a sample, the resulting estimate is biased: $E(s_X^2) \neq \sigma^2$. The expected value of $s_X^2$ is

$$E(s_X^2) = [(N - 1)/N]\, \sigma^2.$$

To see this, use the computational formula $s_X^2 = (\Sigma X_i^2)/N - \overline{X}^2$. The expectation of this is $E(s_X^2) = E[(\Sigma X_i^2)/N - \overline{X}^2] = E[(\Sigma X_i^2)/N] - E(\overline{X}^2) = \Sigma E(X_i^2)/N - E(\overline{X}^2)$. To simplify the first term, recall the definition of a population variance, $\sigma^2 = E(X_i^2) - \mu^2$, so $E(X_i^2) = \sigma^2 + \mu^2$, and $\Sigma E(X_i^2)/N = \Sigma(\sigma^2 + \mu^2)/N = \sigma^2 + \mu^2$. To simplify the second term, recall that the sampling distribution of means has variance $\sigma_{\overline{X}}^2 = E(\overline{X}^2) - \mu^2$, so $E(\overline{X}^2) = \sigma_{\overline{X}}^2 + \mu^2$. Substituting these back, $E(s_X^2) = \Sigma E(X_i^2)/N - E(\overline{X}^2) = (\sigma^2 + \mu^2) - (\sigma_{\overline{X}}^2 + \mu^2) = \sigma^2 - \sigma_{\overline{X}}^2$. Thus, the sample variance is, on average, smaller than the true population variance, $\sigma^2$. Earlier in this chapter it was shown that $\sigma_{\overline{X}}^2 = \sigma^2/N$, so $E(s_X^2) = \sigma^2 - \sigma^2/N = \sigma^2 [(N - 1)/N]$.

The sample variance must be adjusted to remove this bias. Multiplying the sample variance by the fraction $N/(N - 1)$ yields an unbiased estimate: $E\{[N/(N - 1)]s_X^2\} = \sigma^2$. Thus, an unbiased estimate of the population variance can be obtained by using the following formula:

$$s^2 = [N/(N - 1)] \sum (X_i - \overline{X})^2/N = \sum (X_i - \overline{X})^2/(N - 1).$$

That is why the sample variance formula in Chapter 4 divides the sum of squared deviations by the number of cases minus one.

Although $s^2$ is an unbiased estimator of $\sigma^2$, its square root is a biased estimator of the population standard deviation. For example, if the population distribution is normal, then an unbiased estimator of the population standard deviation $\sigma$ is $[(4N - 3)/(4N - 4)]s$. This tends to have minimal effect for large $N$, so such a correction is rarely made.

84

Unbiasedness is a small-sample property. The bias renders the statistic inaccurate when the sample size is small. The correction for bias in the variance is important to use for small samples (i.e., less than 60).

A third desirable property of an estimator is that it be *efficient*. This property involves the relative stability of the estimator over repeated samples. The most efficient unbiased sample statistic (termed the *best unbiased estimator*) would be the one with minimum variance across different samples. Stated in terms of expectations, efficiency requires that E(sample statistic − population parameter)$^2$ be minimized.

Consider first the sample mean as an estimator of the population mean. Say that a large number of samples were taken of size $N$, and the mean was computed for each of those samples to generate a sampling distribution of sample means. We have labeled the variance of this sampling distribution as $\sigma_{\bar{X}}^2$. The sample mean is an efficient estimator of the population mean, because this variance is smaller than that of any other possible estimator of the population mean. For example, the sample median may be a consistent estimator of the population mean, but when the variable has a normal distribution, the sampling distribution of medians has a variance of $(\pi/2)\sigma_{\bar{X}}^2 = 1.5708$ $\sigma_{\bar{X}}^2 > \sigma_{\bar{X}}^2$. Thus, the sample median is a less efficient estimator of the population mean than is the sample mean. The adjusted sample variance is an efficient estimator of the population variance.

The best estimators are consistent, unbiased, and efficient. Some estimators are consistent, but lack the other properties, as is the case in using the sample median to estimate the population mean or in using the unadjusted sample variance to estimate the population variance. Such statistics are fine for very large sample situations but not for small ones. Some estimators are both consistent and unbiased, but are still not the most efficient estimators. The best unbiased estimators are those that are the most efficient, such as the sample mean and the adjusted sample variance.

## APPENDIX A: COMPUTER APPLICATIONS

Single-variable graphs can be obtained from many computer statistics programs, including microcomputer statistics and spreadsheet programs. Bar charts, histograms, and frequency polygons are the most readily available, but modern programs also give pie charts, stem-and-leaf plots, and box plots.

Computer statistics programs invariably provide the common measures of center and spread for metric variables: the mean, variance, and standard deviation. Some also calculate the median, range, and interquartile range.

One problem is that these statistics are usually calculated regardless of the measurement level of the data. The fact that the computer prints them out does not show that they are appropriate; instead the researcher must decide if these statistics are appropriate for the data. In doing so, be sure to graph the variable and examine the shape of the distribution, rather than relying on summary measures.

Typically computer programs and statistical calculators report the sample variance and standard deviation, rather than the population values. Unfortunately, the results are usually not labeled as sample values, leading to occasional confusion in interpreting the computer output.

Most computer programs do not include the EDA-based measures, though some modern microcomputer-based statistics programs do calculate them. The nominal measures of spread reviewed in this book are rarely calculated by computer programs, making them difficult to obtain.

The statistics shown at the bottom of the tables in this monograph were calculated using a program written by the author.

## APPENDIX B: LIST OF MEASURES

Measures are listed in the order they are presented; alternative names for the same measure are listed in parentheses.

### Measures of Center

Mode: mode, crude mode, and refined mode.

Median: median, rough median, and exact median.

Mean: mean, grouped mean, weighted mean, pooled mean, and mean of dichotomous variable.

Other order measures: midextreme (midrange), midhinge, trimean, and biweight.

Other means: trimmed mean, winsorized mean, and midmean; geometric mean, harmonic mean, generalized mean, and quadratic mean.

### Measures of Spread

Numeric: mean deviation (average deviation), population variance, population standard deviation, sample variance, sample standard deviation,

86

pooled variance, variance of dichotomous variable, coefficient of variation (coefficient of relative variation), and Gini's mean difference.

Ordinal: range, interquartile range (midspread), quartile deviation (semi-interquartile range, quartile range), coefficient of quartile variation, median absolute deviation, coefficient of dispersion, and Leik's *D*.

Nominal: variation ratio, index of diversity, index of qualitative variation, entropy, and standardized entropy.

Sampling distributions: variance of sampling distribution of means, standard error of the mean (standard deviation of sampling distribution of means), standard error of a proportion, and sampling error.

## NOTES

1. Note that technically the issue is whether the property underlying the measurements (e.g., heat) has a unit of measurement, so that attitudes are not metric variables because they lack such a unit of measurement.

2. Sometimes numbers are assigned to objects that are fundamentally nonorderable, such as the numbers put on the backs of baseball shirts so that players can be kept track of numerically instead of just by name. However, baseball jersey numbers are not metric, because they are not based on any scale. If the numbers do not correspond to an ordered trait of the objects (and the numbers of baseball players are assigned fairly arbitrarily rather than according to a single ordered property), then the variable is nominal and should not be treated as metric.

3. Some metric scales are neither ratio nor interval. The most common example is the Richter scale that is used to measure the severity of earthquakes. It is a logarithmic scale, set up so that an quake of 7.0 is 10 times as severe as a quake of 6.0, which is 10 times as bad as a quake of 5.0, and so on. Such scales cannot be multiplied by a constant nor have a constant added to them without destroying their properties.

4. When there are large amounts of missing data, it is worth thinking about why the data are missing. In some situations, missing data are meaningful substantively, as when "don't know" is really an intermediate neutral category. In other situations, a systematic process may have produced the missing data. Instead of omitting the missing data, sometimes it may be better to code them at the average of the variable.

5. In addition to measuring the center and spread of a variable, there are statistics to measure the skewness and even the peakedness of a variable's distribution. The sign of the skewness statistic shows whether there is positive or negative skewness. The kurtosis statistic measures how flat or peaked the distribution is.

6. Incidentally, the median itself can be considered an extremely trimmed mean, trimming all but the very central observations. A *broadened median* is a more general form of the median, averaging a few of the central observations (such as the middle three or four or five observations) instead of just using the exact central observation; it also can be thought of as a trimmed mean.

7. The geometric mean cannot be computed if an odd number of the values are negative. That is not a problem in dealing with growth rates, which are always positive—greater than one for positive growth and less than one if deceleration is occurring.

8. The range and interquartile range also can be used on metric data. The median absolute deviation also can be used on metric data, but spread measures based on the median are rarely used with metric data.

9. Many texts report the standard error of the proportion, $\sqrt{p(1-p)/N}$, as its standard deviation. The standard error is discussed in Chapter 5.

10. The negative is used because of a property of logarithms of proportions. Numbers larger than one have positive logarithms and the logarithm of one is zero. Numbers between zero and one, such as proportions, have negative logarithms. Taking the negative of the logarithm thus makes entropy values positive because the negative of a negative number is positive.

11. The base for the logarithms is not critical in this formula—the same numerical result would be obtained regardless of whether the logs are taken to the base 2, the base 10, or the base $e$. Changing from one base to another is a multiplicative relationship, and multiplying the numerator and denominator of the standardized entropy formula by the same multiplicative constant would cancel out.

## REFERENCES

BLALOCK, H. M., Jr. (1972) Social Statistics (2nd ed.). New York: McGraw-Hill.

BORGATTA, E. F., and BOHRNSTEDT, G. W. (1980) "Level of measurement: Once over again." Sociological Methods and Research 9: 147-160.

COULTER, P. B. (1984) "Distinguishing inequality and concentration." Political Methodology 10: 323-335.

GRETHER, D. M. (1976) "On the use of ordinal data in correlation analysis." American Sociological Review 41: 908-912.

HARTWIG, F., and DEARING, B. E. (1979) Exploratory Data Analysis. Beverly Hills, CA: Sage.

HAYS, W. L. (1963) Statistics for Psychologists. New York: Holt, Rinehart and Winston.

IGLEWICZ, B. (1983) "Robust scale estimators and confidence intervals for location," in D. Hoaglin, F. Mosteller, and J. W. Tukey (eds.) Understanding Robust and Exploratory Data Analysis. New York: John Wiley.

JACOBY, W. (1991) Data Theory and Dimensional Analysis. Newbury Park, CA: Sage.

KERLINGER, F. (1973) Foundations of Behavioral Research. New York: Holt, Rinehart and Winston.

KOTZ, S., JOHNSON, N. L., and READ, C. B. (1983) Encyclopedia of Statistical Sciences. New York: John Wiley.

KRIPPENDORFF, K. (1986) Information Theory. Newbury Park, CA: Sage.

LABOVITZ, S. (1970) "The assignment of numbers to rank order categories." American Sociological Review 35: 515-524.

LEABO, D. A. (1972) Basic Statistics. Homewood, IL: Irwin.

88

LEIK, R. (1966) "A measure of ordinal consensus." Pacific Sociological Review 9: 85-90.

MAYER, L. S. (1971) "A note on treating ordinal data as interval data." American Sociological Review 36: 519-520.

MOSTELLER, F., and TUKEY, J. W. (1977) Data Analysis and Regression. Reading, MA: Addison-Wesley.

RAE, D. W., and TAYLOR, M. (1970) Analysis of Political Cleavages. New Haven, CT: Yale University Press.

ROSENBERGER, J., and GASKO, M. (1983) "Comparing location estimators: Trimmed means, medians, and trimean," in D. Hoaglin, F. Mosteller, and J. W. Tukey (eds.) Understanding Robust and Exploratory Data Analysis. New York: John Wiley.

TAYLOR, C., and HUDSON, M. (1972) World Handbook of Political and Social Indicators (2nd ed.). New Haven, CT: Yale University Press.

TUKEY, J. W. (1977) Exploratory Data Analysis. Reading, MA: Addison-Wesley.

VELLEMAN, P. F. (1989) Learning Data Analysis with DATA DESK. San Francisco: Freeman.

VELLEMAN, P. F., and HOAGLIN, D. C. (1981) Applications, Basics, and Computing of Exploratory Data Analysis. Boston: Duxbury.

WALDMAN, L. K. (1976) "Measures of party systems' properties: The number and sizes of parties." Political Methodology 3: 199-214.

WEISBERG, H. F., KROSNICK, J. A., and BOWEN, B. D. (1989) An Introduction to Survey Research and Data Analysis (2nd ed.). Glenview, IL: Scott, Foresman.

YULE, G. U., and KENDALL, M. G. (1968) An Introduction to the Theory of Statistics (14th ed.). New York: Hafner.

# ABOUT THE AUTHOR

*HERBERT F. WEISBERG,* Professor of Political Science at the Ohio State University, received his undergraduate education at the University of Minnesota and his Ph.D. from the University of Michigan. He has been coeditor of the *American Journal of Political Science* and is coauthor of *An Introduction to Survey Research and Data Analysis.* He has written numerous journal articles on such diverse topics as congressional roll-call analysis, scaling methods, party identification, and measures of statistical relationship.